EMPOWERING STORIES FROM FEMALE
VISIONARIES AND ENTREPRENEURS

Voices of Impact Publishing

Copyright © 2023 Voices of Impact Publishing

Foreword by Melanie Wood

All rights reserved. No part of this publication may be reproduced, stored in a retrieval system, or transmitted in any form or by any means, electronic, mechanical, photocopying, recording or otherwise, without the prior written permission from both the copyright owner and publisher.

Disclaimer

All the information, techniques, skills, and concepts contained within this publication are of the nature of general comment only and are not in any way recommended as individual advice. The intent is to offer a variety of information to provide a wider range of choices now and in the future, recognising that we all have widely diverse circumstances and viewpoints. Should any reader choose to make use of the information contained herein, this is their decision and the author and publishers do not assume any responsibilities whatsoever under any condition or circumstances.

Foreword by Melanie Wood

Stories are the most powerful way to have an impact and create a ripple effect in this world.

I have worked with hundreds of women to gain Clarity and Confidence in sharing their stories on stage, on podcasts, at summits and more.

An opportunity came to me early in 2022 to create this book series to share transformational stories of women making an impact.

Sharing my own story in 2020 in a book series and becoming a best-selling author was a game changer. It was time to give this opportunity to other women to make an impact.

It began as something I'd never set out to do; I wasn't born a speaker, a leader or a business owner. Throughout my life, public speaking was never on my horizon. I would avoid it throughout school and my career for almost thirty years – and I did well to avoid it at all costs!

Not setting out to do what I do today came from one of my biggest challenges back in my late teens and early 20s. I was in an abusive marriage where I lost my confidence, voice, certainty, my way in life, and who I was as a woman to the point that I didn't want to be here.

Then one day, a person came along and gave me hope. She reached out to me on a day I couldn't hide anymore what I was going through, and she asked if I was okay, and for once, I said, "No." I knew I had to be ok with using my voice and what would happen next. Her "Impact" on my life is why I'm here today and why I'm so passionate about sharing stories.

As she shared her own story, it gave me hope and the support I needed to leave that marriage. After meeting her and the years that followed, I knew that I was here for more to help other women overcome challenges and find their voice, confidence, and certainty around who they are.

Life changed for me one day 9yrs ago; an opportunity to come to Australia for a year, and something within told me it was time for my adventure to begin, which was what I had been waiting for. Before leaving, I was given the book "The Secret" by Rhonda Byrne. Which changed the way I viewed the world at that moment.

Arriving in Australia, I was ready! Ready to take action! Even though I was scared of being in a new country, I built my new life to stay permanently in Australia.

I wanted to help women like you (that amazing lady reading this book!) have a voice, confidence and clarity. To be able to use your authenticity to create and build a skill set for you and your business and your life or represent your organisation through storytelling, public speaking and communication.

I started my business, Speaking Styles, five years ago and have worked with hundreds of women to help them have a voice in this world to share their story, their message, and their value. To be heard and understood in this world and create a ripple effect, as I believe that stories are how we save lives, make a change, heal ourselves, and help heal other people—giving them hope and permission to do the same.

Building my business for the past 5yrs and working with women is because I knew how to use speaking to create an impact and attract clients. Out of my past experience, I understand what it's like to be in my client's shoes to have empathy and authenticity to work and guide them through sharing their stories.

Doing this work didn't come without its challenges; over 2 years ago, I was 3 days out from living in my car when the big C hit; 6 months before that, I was in debt and struggling to have enough money for rent and food.

I knew these challenges and feelings were part of who I was becoming and where I would be of service in this world—being heartfelt and authentic in everything I do. I didn't get here on my own; yes, I've done the work of the people who have worked with me and guided me over the past 5yrs, and without them, this wouldn't be possible.

I know in my heart that sharing stories is how we create change and save the lives of others, heal ourselves and rise all of us as a collective.

By sharing your story, by communicating your message, by communicating your fantastic work, experience, and expertise, no matter what field you are in. Just like the women in this book are sharing.

At the beginning of the year of 2022, I had this burning desire to create a new opportunity for women to share their transformational stories and IMPACT the world on a larger scale and reach more people. Then one day, only a few months ago, that opportunity came knocking, and Voices of Impact was born, and that desire came to light.

In Volume 1 of Voices of Impact 25 women said yes to being published authors, and it has been an absolute pleasure to publish incredible women's transformational stories. Now continuing the journey in our next volume, shining a light on more incredible woman sharing stories of hope, permission and transformation.

In Volume 2 of Voices of Impact, you will read 20 Visionary Women from around the world sharing TRANSFORMATIONAL stories, creating change and a ripple effect in this WORLD.

Change is within each of us, waiting to be heard and understood.

Ladies, it's your time to step up, step out and lead the change!

The world needs to hear your story!

IMPACT starts with you. Are you with me?

Melanie Wood
Founder, Speaker, Author, Publisher
Voices of Impact Publishing

***

Would you love to have your voice heard to share your story?

Reach out x

melanie@speakingstyles.com.au

Contents

Tiff Babington 1

Lisa Lorna Blair 15

Zilla Carina 33

Lee Cecchin 47

Natasha Coughlan 61

Karen Dawn 75

Melissa Haggarty 93

Elizabeth Hood 107

Sally E Lean 121

Lisa Lonsdale 135

Jordie Lynch 149

Cornelia Macvicar 163

Christine McTaggart 175

Leanne V McVeigh 189

Sue Moore 201

Lara Odushegun 219

Kerstin Rheinlander 233

Lauren Rogers 247

Lauren Smith 263

Melanie Wood 275

Tiff Babington

"The goal of life is to make your heartbeat match the beat of the universe, to match your nature with Nature."
~ *Joseph Campbell*

Lighting the World

Have you ever pondered the bigger questions about life in this universe and on this planet? Did you ever wonder why we are here and what is your purpose?

These questions have interested me from an early age and still do and my vision is to light the world with the wisdom I have learnt and will continue to learn before I leave this current existence for my next energetic experience. I hope by making my knowledge available to everyone, we can transform our lives and as leaders, those of others, and of humanity more generally. I am not the first to deliver these messages - there are many who are sharing and have shared this wisdom, including the ancients

- and I won't be the last - because universal wisdom is not bound by human constructs of time. Some tell it more eloquently than me but I will explain at least some of it from my perspective, without hopefully getting too esoteric, and why it has led me into energy realignment coaching and my mission of transforming leaders through energy mastery, healing and soul realignment.

I believe humanity's purpose is to evolve, to evolve in a way that recognises we are one consciousness with the earth, universe and source, god or spirit - whatever you want to call it - and what we feel, think and do as energetic physical beings has a ripple effect through time, space and dimension. If we can evolve in a way that brings love and light as high vibrational energy into us and we surround ourselves and emanate light unconditionally from our inner being out to the world, we would become extraordinary, and open ourselves to unlimited and infinite possibilities.

As a child I was fascinated with stories of our universe, our planet and humanity's relationship with it and a voracious reader. Any genre would do and very early on I was reading books beyond my years. Books took me to fantastical worlds in the past, present, future and off earth as well as on it. My thirst for knowledge did not change as I grew older. While my parents were non-religious, they had been brought up with Christian values. So as part of my knowledge quest, I explored those values and religion. I took myself off to church, attended bible studies, religious schools and other religious gatherings. At university, I studied comparative religion in addition to political science in an effort to understand our purpose, people and our planet more. I wanted to know what people thought, why they thought it, how their thoughts affected their daily lives, how they connected to themselves individually and collectively, to the earth, to the universe and to spirit. What I didn't fully understand at that time, given the idealism of youth, was how conditioned and programmed we are by our stories, our history, and familial and societal norms and standards, by our DNA and how much these affect how we think, feel and connect to source, each other, our planet and the universe (or not as the case may be).

Nature's powerful role in my life has been constant. Sun, sea and surf are happy childhood memories as are walking in the bush and swimming in rivers. My connection to nature got a bit off centre as a younger adult as I sought material abundance, and to work and play hard.

As the law of attraction would have it, that's exactly what I got, with lots of highs and hard lows filling my life instead, and only intermittent reconnection with nature. Now I find if I'm away from nature for too long, I start getting disconnected from myself.

Similarly, if I don't get outside and put my bare feet on the earth and just breath, I become ungrounded. Humans need to ground and the benefits of being in nature are well-known and manifold for our well-being. If only we took more time to be in and remember our oneness with nature, rather than focussing on our trials and tribulations or getting ahead, we would be better humans all round.

As part of my upbringing, I was taught to work hard because money didn't grow on trees and you needed to be successful. This conditioning was deeply ingrained in me. It is, as I have come to know, a very stressful way to live and stress leads to many related health issues. These days I think of money as energy that will just flow to me if I am living my soul purpose and following my bliss. The desire to serve others was also engrained, driven in much part by injustices I observed in the world. So after university and a few temporary jobs, I embarked on a career of public service, spanning 33 years. Most of this was spent working as a diplomat for New Zealand's foreign service. During this time I became passionate about lifting others out of poverty and specialised in international development and humanitarian issues. Through that work I know I, and others I worked with, made a major difference in the lives of thousands, if not millions, both in times of peace and disaster, and that fills me with a lot of joy.

But development and humanitarian work never ends. Humanity

is an evolving species as is our planet. We are constantly changing - we are born and we die. Natural and man-made disasters are getting more frequent. And because the way our society functions currently, we live in a world which upholds scarcity and lack. We have people with money and people who don't and the people who have money are only a small percentage of the world's population. Much of the world remains in poverty. People die every day from preventable diseases, starvation, malnutrition, and war. Our cultures, religions, and world views divide us. We use resources with little thought for the environment and the damage we are causing Mother Earth and her inhabitants. We litter. We pollute. We abuse, rob from and kill each other. All to advance ourselves. Does life have to be like this? Are we happy because of it?

The pursuit of materialism has in my view taken us away from connection to spirit. Many of us view god as external to ourselves rather than acknowledging we too are made in god's image and are therefore one. We pray and hope for better times and sometimes, we get angry with god for forsaking us. We don't for the most part realise we are the creators our own realities whether consciously or unconsciously, and change our behaviour. The outcomes individually, collectively and for our planet are obvious. We continue to be victims, blaming each other for our woes. We victimise others in an effort to be right or more powerful. We seek to rescue or people please. We live our lives in drama triangles, forgetting we are here to experience our divine design. Or we don't believe in god at all and get disconnected from our own power and that of source. We have been conditioned to forget our true divine nature. Mental health issues and dis-ease abound. Patterns throughout our lives and history continue to repeat themselves because we don't change our energetic vibrations and recognise the universe is expansionist and life within it abundant. Part of our evolution is to learn we can more consciously create our own reality and from a place of love for ourselves, others and the universe. We are an integral part of a universe which is in a constant state of change, renewal and growth.

I, for a long time, pursued a path of material rather than universal abundance. I wanted to feel safe and secure. I wanted to know I would be comfortable in my old age. I married someone who would provide for me and my children. I have three beautiful sons and being a mother is one of my life's greatest achievements. However, I was deeply unhappy in the relationship as I had been with past relationships because while I had material abundance, my emotional and spiritual needs were not met, and I was looking externally for solutions rather than to myself. What I much later realised is I had lost my trust and connection to source and my higher self.

I am a kind and loving person but like a lot of people I have struggled with self love issues. Societal norms have given us a wound that we are not enough or valued just as we are and do not have enough. Wounds from childhood were also deep as were a number of ancestral ones carried in my DNA and from past lives. I created a whole lot more emotional trauma in adulthood through self-betrayal by not putting myself first, not understanding how to process my emotions and suppressing them sometimes to the point of physical, mental and spiritual illness, not being clearer on my values and boundaries, not speaking my truth, and doing lots of self-sabotage. To all intents and purposes, people looking at me would have thought I had it all - good career which included two diplomatic postings to Vanuatu and Rome, a successful husband, a lovely house, nice possessions, overseas trips, beautiful children, good friends, but I was not happy in essence and I couldn't understand why.

A midlife crisis beset me - I didn't know what I wanted, where I was going but I knew I didn't want to be in a life and relationship that was making me depressed. And so, as I have throughout my life, and being an only child, decided again to pursue a path of independence, freedom and take back my power. I moved out, bought a house and dreamed of moving offshore as part of my job. But my children were too young to leave and my husband wouldn't let me take them with me. So I stayed in New Zealand until my youngest was 13 and ready for college. I was fortunate my career took me to amazing places all over the world and I have been blessed to go to the Pacific, Asia, Africa, Latin America, and Europe with my work and for pleasure. For that I am very grateful because it meant I kept learning and experiencing. That was for me a big part of the love of my job and life in general, and got me through darker moments. The people I got to meet and places in the world I got to see were energising especially seeing how others lived and the projects we were doing that were making a difference in their lives. Travel is something I encourage everyone to do as it broadens horizons and our humanity. I will continue to travel until I am no longer able as there is so much more to experience in our beautiful world.

Over the course of my career, I was involved in the building of hospitals, schools and utilities, introducing new agricultural techniques, education, health, justice, security systems, and assisting in times of disaster both environmental and man made. I worked with governments, politicians, regional, multilateral and non-government organisations, and the private sector. I learnt a lot about how the world works, how we interact with each other, how we use resources on our planet, and how we present ourselves as humans as a result.

My career also led me into leadership positions where I managed people and resources. At first I felt out of my depth as I was managing in some instances people older and more experienced. I also thought because I was in an environment where there was lots of competition to shine, I needed to manage in a way that was more directive than felt comfortable. Over time and with support from some good managers, mentors and coaches, I realised I could lead in a way that felt authentic, and right for me as a human being. Now I lead from the heart and always try to come from a place of compassion and fairness. It has given me great pleasure to observe how people respond positively to that style of leadership and grow both professionally and personally as a result.

But my life hasn't always been consciously heart-led or an easy journey and a couple of times I have even considered checking out when it has gotten really dark. I have learnt a lot of lessons and some very hard ones but lessons are part of the soul's journey and until I learnt them, I found they tended to repeat themselves. Lessons are part of our conscious evolution and the soul contract we sign for up for coming into this incarnation. They make us the human beings we are and I am very grateful for both the lessons as well as the many blessings I've had.

So how did I make the change from being a diplomat to energy realignment coach? The catalyst was a spiritual awakening during my last post on Tonga as New Zealand's High Commissioner. I got very sick with a mystery illness and was bedridden for almost six weeks. My awakening took me to an online conscious creation summit and an akashic record reading which was life-changing as I finally understood my soul purpose. For the three years since, I have been on a voyage of self-rediscovery through energy mastery, healing and soul realignment with the support of some very good mentors, coaches, courses, and self-reflection time. There has been a lot of dark night of the soul moments as I took responsibility for being the creator of my reality and reprogrammed my beliefs, emotions and actions to better align with universal wisdom including who I am at soul level. I have learnt to reconnect with source and my higher self through meditation, and trusting my heart and gut not just my head, and to love myself wholeheartedly and unconditionally. My voyage also made me realise my life's service has always been about transforming lives and applying what I have learnt. But if I truly wanted to make a difference to humanity then I needed to share that wisdom more directly through teaching and coaching others from a place of true authenticity.

So here are some universal wisdoms I have learnt so far. The universe is abundant and unlimited. Everything is energy and constantly changing. As energetic beings, our soul purpose is to experience our divinity through physicality. We attract the energy we emit so it is important to consciously focus on what we want (not what we don't want), why we want it, and how we want to feel (eg joy). We have free will to create our reality - no one else is responsible. We have everything we need right here, right now, as we are one with the universe/source. We need to trust and surrender to source, our higher selves, our soul purpose and life's flow. If we aren't in flow, we can always change our state by acknowledging our emotions are our GPS for life, and following our bliss and what feels better and more free. We need to have dark moments to learn and make a conscious and free choice to be in the light. We can heal karmic blocks and restrictions we have created in this life, past lives, ancestral lives and when we do, we can evolve our individual souls, collective consciousness, and heal karma for future generations. Forgiveness is freedom. Our connection to source is through our hearts not our minds. We will return to source when we pass and be transmuted into another energetic form of our choosing thereafter.

Humans really are extraordinary beings. We can choose to end our suffering, evolve and master our energy. We can rewrite our stories at any time. We can transform. So if you are struggling in life, you are stuck or you want to make a change for the better, I can support you. As a start, here are my top ten tips for energy mastery and staying in the light that my clients have told me they have found useful.

They are not rocket science and some are easier said than done but if applied can create a whole new and better reality to what you might be experiencing right now:

- Love yourself first and foremost
- Start your day with appreciation and positive energy
- Practice mindfulness and conscious awareness
- Set goals, have greater purpose, take action
- Always be open and connected to universal abundance, wisdom, and possibilities

- Move and fuel your body for well-being
- Count your blessings and your lessons
- Take time to relax, sleep and have fun
- Nurture healthy relationships

For more support on how to implement these tips and transform your life, you can connect to my website, Facebook and Instagram pages, or book a free 30-minute discovery call.

My vision is to light the world through transforming leaders lives through energy mastery, healing and soul realignment. Are you ready to transform your life and remember the universal wisdom available to all of us? What if we could as human beings, individually and collectively, manifest a reality that comes from better connecting to ourselves, source, unconditional love, light, and nature? What if we as leaders could better role model what that looks like, and lead others into the light and empower humanity to remember our brilliance as light beings? What if we could be more extraordinary, abundant, unlimited, and live as one consciousness? What if globally, we were all awakened to universal wisdom? I believe our heartbeats can match the beat of the universe and I know a growing number of you do too.

So bring in light, stay in light, be light and transmit light, and watch your life, and that of humanity, our planet and the universe transform for the better. Together we can light the world.

About the Author

Tiff Babington is an energy realignment coach. Her mission is "Lighting the World". Drawing on her professional and personal experience as a former senior diplomat, people and organisational change leader, and international development specialist, Tiff supports leaders in their fields to transform their lives through energy mastery, healing and soul realignment. Tiff provides intuitive inspiration, insights, and powerful tools, to those wanting to become more successful, empowered, and embody their soul's true purpose.

Tiff works 1:1 with clients, in person or online. She also provides organisational and group coaching. Tiff integrates universal wisdom from the akashic records, the 7 essential laws, channelling, energy healing, the emotion code, and mindfulness into her coaching practice. Tiff loves to spend time with family and friends, and travel. She has three adult sons and a granddaughter, and is semi-retired in Opotiki, New Zealand.

Email: contactme@tiffbabington.com
Facebook: @TIFFBABINGTON
Website: www.tiffbabington.com

Lisa Lorna Blair

And the Beat Goes On!!!

"How can you mend a broken heart?"

My finger traced lightly over the soft skin covering my heart space. I stood, in the shower, tears streaming down my face, holding back the screams of fear.

I let the tears come.
Release was inevitable.
Needed.
And when it finally came....
It felt good.

That cold Winter's morning I was saying goodbye to my heart valve.

The beautiful valve that had served my body for over five decades.

The valve that had pumped the blood through my heart all my life, allowing me to walk, run, roller-skate, play hockey, netball and basketball in my childhood.

It had been with me through three healthy pregnancies and three natural childbirths.

Then in my forties, that little valve gave my body the energy and exhilaration to enter two mini triathlons, bungee jump off a bridge and leap out of a plane in a tandem skydive in New Zealand, climb thousands of steps at temples in South East Asia, ascend the Eiffel Tower in Paris and enjoying climbing numerous castles and the Wallace Monument in Scotland.

A valve that supported me through decades of trauma, creation, fun, grief and loss, joy and elation, agony and ecstasy.

So many times in my life when my heart could have failed me, it did not.

So many times where my breath was weak and shallow and my lungs were aching, there should have been an "ah ha" moment that signalled something was wrong.

I just thought when I was struggling for breath that I needed to work on my fitness. When my heart was racing out of control, I gave up caffeine, as I believed that was the cause. I released weight, became fitter, turned to more holistic and natural ways of eating and living.

I hadn't known.

My mother hadn't known.

Yet I look back now and ask myself if we had known, would I have done all those wonderful things and experienced those incredible moments and memories?

So, I am grateful for it.

All of it.

You see, by the time my "broken heart" was discovered, I was fully surrounded and supported by both the expert medical professionals and the holistic carers who could support my journey.

I was happy, healthy and well, safe, loved and secure.

All this tumbled through my mind on that cold morning, as the warm water and steam enveloped me.

"Goodbye little valve, thank you for being with me all this time," I said.

I caressed and thanked the skin across my chest. I let the soap glide across it smooth and safe just one – last – time.

In 12 hours that beautiful unblemished skin surface would be cut open with a scalpel and scarred for life. Where once there was smooth skin there would be an open wound and then a knotty pink scar.

I was alone with the enormity of these thoughts and it was time to cry. Deep, guttural cries of anguish and release.

The following day my husband kissed me goodbye at the doorway of the cardiac surgery wards.

I sat with a pen in my hand waiting to sign the consent documents as my surgeon gently explained that I needed to be aware that, even though these operations take place daily, there is still somewhere between 1-3 percent chance of fatality. My exhale of breath seemed very loud in that moment. But, I leaned into everything that I had been doing for the months leading up to this moment.

All the inner work and embodiment that had become second nature. And in that moment I placed my trust in the 97 to 98 per cent chance that I WOULD BE emerging on the other side later that day, and thanked my surgeon for his honesty, smiled at him and signed my name.

As they wheeled me into the operating theatre I took in every sight and sound.

The "space age" looking equipment, the sterile environment and the smiling, friendly faces of the anaesthetist, a nurse, assistants that seemed to appear from everywhere. Next came a peculiar ice cold feeling as the line in my arm filled with drugs and my animated conversation in response to questions about my kids and grand-kids, where I live and what I "do for a living", and how I help people, drew to an abrupt halt. The talented team swung into action.

Now you already know the story has a happy ending, or you would not be reading this..

Today, I am here writing this chapter on the other side of the successful Edwards Inspiris Aortic Valve replacement surgery.

During my post-op hospital stay, my husband brought fresh juices, home made soups and 4 litres of 9.5pH electrolysed reduced water every day. I was up and about walking and began to heal so quickly, they sent me home days earlier than anticipated. A six-week recovery at home followed and then another six weeks of rehabilitation at my local hospital gym.

I am happy, grateful, blessed and living healthier than ever.

Physically, the healing is evident. My body is functioning so well now. My lungs are back to full capacity, the new valve has settled in brilliantly and blood is pumping powerfully around my body, just as it is meant to do. All my life I was missing one vital piece and didn't even know.

It is obvious that I am healthy and well – it is so clear for me, my loved ones, my friends. And yet, emotionally, the healing of a literal broken heart has been a far bigger journey.

And in many ways, is still ongoing.

I recall watching the 2020 documentary "How can you mend a broken heart" about the Bee Gees, told, for the most part, through the memories of the surviving brother, Barry. The titular tune played as he reminisced towards the end, saying something along the lines of, if he could, he would trade all the fortune, fame, number one hits, the movies and money if he could just have his family back together, safe and whole again. His voice trembled and his face was etched with pain. Barry's heart was so very broken, many times, but he had to move on. We all have to move on.

Through pain, through devastating loss, through grief. We all navigate these experiences in life and our nervous system absorbs them all.

The documentary was a beautiful tribute to his family and his love for them, even when they were estranged.

That song poses the question - "How CAN you mend a broken heart?"

The simple response is, you cannot.

Yes, a physical heart can be "mended" by a surgeon, but emotionally? You cannot ever fully come back to how things were. But the good news it that you CAN gently heal the emotions, work through them, recover and rise again.

You can move through the heartbreak.
You can heal parts of you on a soul level.
And through it all become more resilient, more loving, more forgiving, more compassionate.

Did I always know all this?

No, of course not. It has been a journey!

I carry a physical scar, neatly hidden away between my breasts. Most would never even know that I have been through the rigours of open-heart surgery and its after effects. But probe beyond the physical and get to the emotional side, the evidence is there.

When we navigate heartbreak of loss, betrayal, abandonment and grief... there are (in most cases) no physical scars to show.

However, we DO carry the emotional fallout, trauma and mental wounds. And it can last many years. So whilst I move well, feel good, breathe strongly and listen with wide-eyed joy and wonder to the "lub-dub" sound of a healthy heartbeat now, for the first time in my life, there are still moments that catch me out emotionally.

The layers peel back, triggered by a range of things. Sometimes activated by a specific moment, words, a memory, a photograph or an experience.

Other times it catches me completely by surprise and I only know it when I realise I am holding my breath, or the cascades of emotion pummel me like the relentless force of being dumped by a surprise wave in the ocean.
What I have personally learned – the hard way (of course!) - is that the more I hold on, or bottle it up, the bigger the toll it takes. So now, I find the release. And I invite you to explore the same. My tools are gratitude, meditation, prayer, joy, grounding in nature, movement. Raising my vibration.

I cry when I need to cry.
I slow down when I need to slow down.
I choose my emotional reaction to situations and people, with care and thoughtfulness.

But it takes time.
It takes "owning your shit"
It takes forgiveness and
It takes compassion

We are spiritual beings having a human experience and we won't always get it right.

We flail about, doing our best with what we know and with what life throws at us. And we can look at everything we've been dealt with through the lens of anger, fear and unforgiveness, or we can look through the lens of love. I choose love.

I was in my forties when I was diagnosed with a heart murmur, during a chance check up with a random GP. By then I had already had my babies, already done so many adventurous things. There was no real cause for panic or concern from that diagnosis, but even so, I made lifestyle and health choices to support my journey, hoping that would support a turn-around. Thankfully, I didn't have to do this phase of the journey alone.

I had married my best friend and soul mate as the sun rose over Mt Agung in Bali, went on holidays and adventures with him, became a proud grandmother to twin girls and celebrated turning 50.

It wasn't until we had moved 3000kms away from family and friends to start a new life in a whole new part of Australia that we discovered the aortic valve was actually bicuspid, meaning, only two leaflets existed, rather than the standard three, to open and close and allow blood flow to pump through the aorta.

My heart had likely been "broken" all my life and yet, no one knew.

On an emotional and energetic level though, I knew. Oh how I knew!

And as the journey towards my eventual surgery unfolded, more and more aspects came to light.

Getting to know and understand the head and heart connection on such a powerful emotional level has helped me heal far more than just the outward physical aspects.

There has been deep "inner work" and embodiment, emotional healing, forgiveness and trauma release.

When I stepped into my new career working online as an affiliate marketer and conscious entrepreneur, I began to meet more and more coaches, healers and leaders who were leading people through trauma release, spiritual awakenings and embodiment.

I know now that this was no accident. I was divinely guided and led.

As I began my own internal and emotional journey, working with some incredible and gifted healers, we began to probe the many times where I was dealt the blows that literally "broke my heart".

From being an "unplanned pregnancy" at a time when unwed mothers were very much frowned upon, to growing up knowing that my birth father rejected me and abandoned my mother and I whilst I was in utero.

To the heartbreak of a stepfather who initially took me in as his own, adopted me and gave me his name, but then seemingly "lost interest" when my brother was born.

More heartbreak as my parents fought over money and raising their children/stepchildren with very different values around family, religious beliefs and principles.

The heartbreak of my father betraying my mother and us having to pack up and "run away" to my beloved grandpa for sanctuary and then continuously move to various rentals, as she navigated being a single mother, working full time and trying to keep my brother and I safe, well and provided for.

My heart was breaking for her and watching her trying to keep it together.

My heart was breaking for not having a "normal childhood" and a family unit like the ones my friends seemed to have.

Then came the heartbreak that so many of us know well – teenage crushes that ended badly, including the discovery that a long-term boyfriend was sleeping with one of my best friends behind my back.

Two rushed engagements that created emotional upheaval, then eventually getting married and having children while I was still very young, convinced that if I built my own "happy family" and poured my heart into making someone else happy, went to church and followed what the Bible said, life would be good and no one could hurt me.

On the outside it looked picture perfect.

The reality? Not so much.

Narcissistic family members could not and would not accept me, no matter how hard I tried. The over-anxious people pleaser in me was not just birthed and activated in my twenties and thirties, she went into over-drive.

I wanted, no, I NEEDED these people to love, accept me, support me!!!

Instead, I was laughed at, criticised at every turn, dismissed and treated with condescension.

My home making skills were sneered at.
My faith was laughed at.
My parenting was critiqued.

Even choosing my first daughter's name was a bone of contention. It was "too unique" and I was told I should stick with something simple and use my sister in law's middle name instead. I stuck to my guns and was probably never forgiven for it.

Family members who should have been a major part of my children's formative years all stepped away and wanted nothing to do with them.

When my then husband tried and failed at various careers and ventures, it was somehow always "my fault".

We kept moving to different towns, leaving friends, family and support networks behind us, going backwards financially and re-starting each time he had a new idea. We were so naïve, so young and were not facing our own trauma. The cracks began to appear.

It was perhaps no surprise when our marriage eventually did dissolve that, even though he was the one who walked away, all the blame, finger pointing and accusations were poured upon me.

Rather than asking for the truth, some family and "friends" simply took a totally distorted version and gave that credibility. I could have spoken up, but for decades I had been silenced over so many other things. My voice was lost. A closed off throat chakra, thyroid issues and a cacophony of self-doubt and poor self-image came to light years later.

At the time I just allowed the mistruths to circulate.

Allowed myself to be treated poorly.

And that's on me. I let that happen. I just had no energy to fight it anymore.

However, this is not where I remain, as these painful moments and memories are simply just facets of the journey.

I look at those moments – the good, the bad, the painful, the sad – with fondness and gratitude now, not bitterness and certainly not regret.

I have three incredible daughters, all now beautiful grown women with loving partners and I have twin granddaughters who are the light of our lives.

There are trusted, true and loyal friends in my circle who have supported and held me in the brokenness. I have so much love and friendship in my life that is genuine, pure and doesn't come with any requirements or expectations.

I can be ME, authentically. The weird, wonderful, sensitive, empathic, creative, generous, heartfelt, spiritual and giving person that I have always craved to be.

Life experiences and heartbreak teach us so much. We can choose to focus on what we "lose", or we can focus on what we actually "gain".

The resilience, strength, empowerment.

I have gratitude for the journey and appreciation for where I am now. I count those blessings daily.

I don't dwell on betrayal or verbal abuse. I am not defined nor consumed by what broke my heart.
We get to choose.

Choose fear, choose heartbreak, choose loss OR choose to see all those things through forgiveness and through the lens of love.

I know now that I was divinely guided and led to a life beyond the pain. A gateway was created for me, even though it was hard to see at the time.

To be living now in a beautiful community, surrounded by love, light, beautiful energy and empowerment. And incredible weather!

To be in a deeply loving and committed marriage with a man who is my best friend and soul mate, who empowers, protects and believes in me and tells me daily I am loved, needed and inspirational.

To have the most beautiful soul connection of my life.

To have left a decades-long corporate media career of meeting deadlines, hustle and grind to now being abundant, free, getting paid to BE ME through the gift of affiliate marketing and a global community of conscious entrepreneurs who celebrate with me, share inspiration, mentoring and empowerment.
To have manifested our glorious dream home acreage property (in the midst of a snap lockdown!) and be living in a paradise of nature and beauty.

To be a best-selling author, business leader, gratitude goddess, manifestation muse and entrepreneur.

To be stepping into my healing gifts, coaching, mentoring and heart-centred creativity.

To have a global six-figure business and be living peacefully, happily, full of vitality, wellness and health and daily showing other women (and men!) all over the world exactly how to create a life they love too.

To be able to book global travel and never have to ask for "time off" to take those trips. To book "goddess days" in the middle of a week, because I know my self-care cup needs filling.

To support family members whenever they need help.

How can you mend a broken heart?

You fill that heart with gratitude, love and joy and then you take it and spread it everywhere.

Sprinkle that "magic dust" wherever you go and watch your life transform. And better still, as your own beat goes on, watch with pure joy as that rhythm attracts a harmonious vibration.

Before you know it, so many others will be beating in unison with you!

About the Author

Lisa Lorna Blair is a wife, mother, daughter and grandma living her best life in her dream home on the Sunshine Coast hinterland with her soul mate husband Kevin and their two ragdoll cats Gatsby and Amadeus. The former award-winning journalist and social media manager, actress and director is now a Gratitude Goddess, Manifestation Muse, cacao addict, theta healer, coach, mentor and high vibe cheerleader. Yep! Lisa wears many hats, and wouldn't have it any other way.

She is also an empath, ambivert, best-selling author and global conscious entrepreneur with a six-figure affiliate marketing business who eats plant-based food, drinks 9.5 alkalised ionised water and lives abundantly mentoring others to be, do and have it all.

Instagram and Facebook: @lisalornablair
Join her free Facebook community: The Manifestation Muse Movement: bit.ly/ManifestationMuseFBgroup

Zilla Carina

My story begins in southern Sweden in 1965.

My Swedish roots go back as far as currently traceable, and I often romanticise I am of noble and strong Viking stock. How else could I have made it through this lifetime so far? Indeed, I believe I have a connection to a Swedish King along the line and I often think how funny it is that most people don't know where we come from or who we are.

Both my parents worked in the airline industry and travelled extensively. In the early 1970's, about to move to Denmark for Dad's work, Mum received a call from the Australian Consulate in Stockholm. They had applied and been accepted for a program called "Assisted Passage", promoted by the Australian Government. Mum couldn't wait for Dad to wake up from his night shift sleep! They had totally forgotten about it and had two weeks to confirm with the Consulate if they were going to move or not. After some short conversations, they decided to do it, and shortly after on our way to Melbourne, Australia. My parents deemed that the 'mandatory' two years stay was worth the adventure!

And what an adventure it was! My brother and I learnt to speak basic English on the plane trip over. We arrived at the Immigrant Hostel in Melbourne. There was no kitchen in our small unit, so every day we dined in the cafeteria for breakfast, lunch, and dinner. It was so gross - as you walked into the cafeteria, there was a type of 'foyer' which absolutely stunk of humid warm vomit! I have no idea where it came from and the smell inside slightly improved but thankfully, it was not the same stench. All I remember is that it was ordinary bland food and I quickly learnt to hold my breath every time I had to go near the place!

Within months Dad and friend/colleague Ed, found work with a helicopter company in Sale, near 90 Mile Beach. Our two families bought a caravan each and off we went. For six months, we called our caravan home, parked by a river where we caught eels. Coming from city life in Sweden, the wildlife was exciting albeit a little scary at the beginning with kangaroos, a myriad of new sounds, and goodness knows what else. We lived in Victoria a total of eight years. We had a two-year sojourn back to Sweden, and that's a story for another time.

After five primary schools and one high school, we moved from Melbourne to the beautiful Gold Coast. Mum and Dad had finally found their "paradise" and Dad scored a job at Brisbane

Airport. I attended two additional high schools before commencing University and absolutely loved the new relaxed lifestyle and people.

After finishing my degree, I worked as a Scientific Officer and Environmental Consultant. I then became the first female Workplace Health and Safety Advisor in the Queensland Government (QG) and spent most of the 1990's working in various QG Senior/Management roles.

In 1992, I married my first husband for all the wrong reasons, like many women do. By putting my own feelings second, I didn't have it in me to say no to his proposal and justified to myself that after all we were best friends, and I was determined to make it work. We were living in Sweden at the time, as I has wanted to move 'home' so I could decide for myself where 'home' truly was in the world.

After almost two years, I received a call from a work colleague with an offer interview for a management position in Brisbane. It was approaching the Nordic winter, and I was not looking forward to the short, freezing cold days ahead. Two weeks later, I had resigned from my job as a relief teacher at a Swedish primary school and was on a plane back to Brisbane to start a new adventure once again. My husband remained for a further three months to complete the lease on our apartment and his Swedish language course.

What was so challenging, heart-breaking, and soul-destroying in my marriage was that my husband seemed unable to take responsibility for his psychological well-being, and I found myself constantly on edge and walking on eggshells. I reached out to him but it was met with a wall - the roller doors would come crashing down. When I think back to his quiet, withdrawn demeanour, perhaps he was suffering depression. I was a talker, he wasn't, and it became such a difficult and uncomfortable environment to live in. I buried myself in work to cope.

By the end of the 1990's I found myself at a major crossroads. My marriage was off track and work became lacklustre. I had also lost a dear friend to an overdose which shattered my soul with grief. Unfortunately, my husband was unable to be 'there' for me to lean on. The call to take some action was strong, I knew I had to do something…. anything! On a whim, I decided to tag along with my best friend for a life changing hike in Tasmania, the Overland Track. Whilst enveloped by a beautiful mountain environment, it was a gruelling 95 kilometre undertaking. No running water, no mattresses on the plywood bunk beds and we had to carry in and carry out absolutely everything. I had never done a big hike like that before. I was totally unprepared; I even borrowed a shitty backpack that was so uncomfortable and kept slipping and sliding as I walked. I experienced massive challenges on every level, physically, emotionally, and spiritually. Alas, I had the realisation that I needed to make some big life decisions if I was going to create and live a life that I would love.

I realised I had been pretending for many years. I 'believed' my life was great, but I was so busy trying to ensure everybody else's happiness, it was a rude shock to discover and acknowledge my own deep sorrow. This later showed up to be a pattern of mine that I needed to deal with and to own my own happiness. The conversation that ended my first marriage was by far the most difficult conversation I ever had up to that time. Little did I know what was yet to come. As I awakened, I realised the suffering I had generated in both of our lives was because I didn't connect with my strength and listen to my heart's intuition. I should have spoken my truth in the first place. Ah, hindsight!

Later that year, with a year leave of absence from work, I left to travel the world to visit family and friends dotted across the globe. Unbeknown to me at the time, it triggered a rite of passage that would ultimately change, amaze, and profoundly challenge me for the next twenty years.

In New Zealand, I met a guy through a mutual friend with whom I felt I had met before on some mysterious soul level. My feelings for him were beyond words and I truly believed he was "the one". We dated and were soon living together. I was absolutely besotted and fell head over heels in love. Unfortunately, my love goggles were so blurred I missed all the red flags popping up more frequently than I cared to admit or even acknowledge. He was a master of psychological abuse, I had never cried so much and felt so alone in a relationship as I did with him.

Four years in a row, I would find myself making an annual departure from him and our home. Each time he would convince me to come back with flowers, champagne and promises of change and doing better, so I'd return. The 'cycle of violence' had commenced, and I didn't even know. Each time I returned, after circa three months, he would let me down, I would forgive him, making excuses for his behaviour, and this toxic cycle would continue until I'd leave yet again.

It wasn't until I fell pregnant and we married that the physical abuse came. There were unseen bruises, a slap here and there, and the pushing and shoving became more frequent as my pregnancy progressed. I kept making excuses for his behaviour and blamed 'myself'. After my beautiful girl arrived, it began to escalate on both the physical and psychological fronts. I remember only weeks after she was born, he forcefully grabbed her from me and proceeded to chant over and over "Mummy's crazy, it's just going to be you and me". I was beyond petrified for her safety. This set the tone for the remaining time I was with him. I was so anxious, scared and felt totally helpless.

I had no idea where to turn or what to do, my parents and

siblings lived overseas and out of reach. I felt ashamed, embarrassed, lost and my self-esteem was sub-zero. There was not a shred of inner strength left. I truly believed I 'was' going insane and his narrative was, "who's going to believe you, it's my word against yours!" It wasn't until he had me pinned to the ugly purple leather sofa threatening to kill me, for the second time, that I started waking up. I was so scared and concerned for our safety that I didn't sleep before I was sure he was asleep. There was no way I wanted my girl to grow up thinking this behaviour was "normal", and I knew I had to get us both out in one piece. But how?

Looking back, I wish I'd known it was okay to reach out for help. It was my girl's fifteen-month health check when the nurse bailed me up and said, "So, Zilla…. tell me, what's really going on?" She knew or could feel my distress and I broke down and everything came flooding out. To this day I will be forever grateful for her understanding and guidance to give me a touch of sanity back and tell me it was imperative to be safe and to take steps to move forward and away from this environment.

My first port of call was the Smith Family, where I started my healing journey and even attempted couples counselling to try and save our marriage. I finally acknowledged that there was no changing the spots on this leopard, so I spent the next few months gaining my strength and planning a safe exit. I made no waves, became very quiet and subdued, until he started shoving and slapping my baby. I vividly recall the morning, I found myself crouching and cornered in the kitchen with my arms wrapped around my girl, waiting for the fist in the back of my head. I was terrified. That was it! I quickly found a place for us to live, got in touch with a lawyer and a few friends to help with the exit. During the last few days, I would smuggle out toys, clothing and a few special heirlooms, the bare necessities.

I had arranged a "play date" for my girl - she was safe with a friend, while I returned with two very kind male friends to pick up a sofa bed, so we'd have something to sleep on. This was when I gave him the letter telling him we were leaving, and he lost it!. He physically dragged me into the house (I had bruises down the whole left side of my body). Somehow, I wriggled loose while he was locking the door on the guys helping me. I yelled out to start the van and scrambled out through a window. I'm trembling as I write this, so many things are coming back, but I'm so grateful I got out and stayed out! This event was later dubbed "The Great Escape".

The years that ensued came with stalking, threats, several court proceedings, and a feeling of being "in jail" as all my, and my little family's freedoms were taken away. We had to apply to the Court if we were going to slightly step outside the confines of the Parenting Court Order due to my ex's controlling behaviour. The fear I felt for my daughter's safety and well-being was indescribable and the self-preservation strategies I implemented somehow managed to keep me going and absolutely saved me. There were a few close calls and believing that everyone would be better off if I wasn't around anymore. During this time, I met my third husband and had my gorgeous boy. I lost both my parents at this time as well, and that made life even more challenging. I took to learning the guitar and sought out support for my inner health via meditation and hypnosis. Fortunately, I found my mentor and mediation master, Tom Cronin, joined his beautiful community and I will be forever grateful for his ongoing guidance and friendship.

Being in such a deep state of stress and depression for such a long period of time took its toll and I will be forever grateful for the ongoing support by those closest to me. It was a long and tough journey, and it wasn't until I heard Vishen Lakhiani of Mindvalley saying loud and clear that we all have a "choice"! It felt like I had been slapped in the face! We choose what and how we feel. I had been telling myself that I had "no choice" and "I am stuck" for so long I'd forgotten this important fact! I took this information and made a CHOICE to be UN-STUCK and began my journey "home". There was so much going on around me at the time, it didn't occur to me that I was in pre-menopause - experiencing hot flushes, brain fog, mood swings and so much more.

I have since realised how much this also significantly impacted my own inner health and well-being. Hence, my passion for bringing the whole menopause journey into mainstream conversation and shedding light on all the things we can do to save our sanity, lives, and marriages.

After fourteen years, the Court Order dissolved, and I could finally start to see freedom becoming real. I felt myself have breakthrough after breakthrough and with the support of my husband, family, and several counsellors, I regained my self-worth, confidence, and courage to step into my true self again. We had planned to move to Australia from the get-go and had bought a home that we would eventually move into. Things were really coming together - my daughter came home full-time, and it was fabulous to finally be free of all the shackles and restrictions and move forward with our lives.

Then came COVID. Shit! We were in the process of setting up our home in Australia and had plans to move in time for my daughter to finish, and our son to start, high school in Australia. The ensuing obstacles came and went. My son and I moved to Australia in late 2020, and my husband and daughter stayed behind whilst she finished high school. The prolonged shutdown of New Zealand played havoc with being able to see each other, but once the border openings were announced, my husband booked and flew over immediately. I was so excited but stressed to the max, worried about whether he would like our new home, where we lived and so on.

After a few days, he said he totally understood why I was so happy and passionate about living in the area we had chosen. I finally relaxed, let go of my worries and was so looking forward to us all being together as a family again, starting fresh and starting a new adventure.

Since then, things took a drastic turn for the worse. That story is long and will be expanded on in my upcoming book called "The Scars". So, now it's just my son and I living in Australia and the rollercoaster ride of pain, anxiety, grief, and realisations over the last year has taken its toll once again. He made the choice to change paths, it was up to me to choose to accept that and move on with my own path.

The great news is I have done the work, made the changes I needed to make and I'm so excited to have had the chance to finally grow into the real me! Since my late teens, I have always wanted to be of service to others and now, I'm fully ready and equipped to do this in a big way. My past choices have got me to where I am today and have taught me resilience, self-belief and the ability to bounce back after setbacks. It has become second nature for me to see a path forward for myself and my clients. I am looking forward to help guide many more clients on their journeys.

Two questions I ask myself when life is challenging:
1. *What is it I'm pretending not to know?*
2. *Am I letting life happen to me…. or for me?*

It's incredible how much these two questions can pivot your whole mindset! They have saved me on numerous occasions. Go on, give it a try!

My passion to guide pre-menopausal women has grown exponentially over the last year, specifically education, information and with open hearted conversations. Seeing my sisters around the world in pain and experiencing so much grief, I am called to be of service to guide their own relief, rediscovering joy and a sense of normality during the menopause experience. It truly is a new beginning and magical time for us all.

I am determined to bring the menopause journey into mainstream conversation with guided coaching and public speaking to show there is an instinctive path to navigate the transition. I am collaborating with fellow menopause coaches across the globe championing the same cause, reframing perceptions, and bringing more understanding and empathy around the reality of menopause.

About the Author

Zilla Carina is a Swedish Australian Menopause and Empowerment Coach. For more than three and half decades, she has successfully mentored and trained over one thousand people in a variety of professional and personal disciplines. Zilla specialises in illuminating the journey for women seeking to THRIVE through menopause. Her cutting-edge practices restore balance, confidence and courage, whilst debunking the myriad of menopause misconceptions. Zilla is an exceptional and experienced life coach, passionate about helping people find clarity and success. She empowers those willing to take responsibility for living consciously, in order to transform and up-level their lives.

Zilla is a Certified Hypnotherapist, Time-Line Therapist, Neurolinguistic Programming Coach, with a Degree in Environmental Science. Zilla enjoys spending time with her kids, surfing, swimming, writing, making music, travelling and embracing every adventure.

Email: hello@menopausecoaching.online
FB/Insta: Zilla Carina
Website: www.menopausecoaching.online

Lee Cecchin

The Girl From the Bush

My mum was 16 years old when she had me; she was still a child herself; I'm the oldest of four girls, mum divorced when I was four years old. When she met the man that would raise us along with his 2 sons (my brothers). He would treat us as his own, we thought he was the best; he would take us camping and out into the bush, trapping rabbits fishing and yabbying; we had chickens and a whole range of pets. We grew our own food, and mum was happy, laughing until they both started drinking, this is when he would change, and his secret came out.

They would stay up late having parties regularly where they would both drink, causing them to argue all the time. He had a mean streak and very abusive when he drank, he would take it out on mum. He and mum would argue all the time, which would set him off, then he would beat mum up and several times, he would try to take her life on many occasions. I would try to stand up to him though this meant I would suffer the consequences, as I was the eldest, I would be his target.

I would run to the police station to get help but they never helped. People would always believe the adult, and everyone would think or see what they wanted to see because when you see them sober, they are picture-perfect.

I took on the role of the parent cooking meals and cleaning, and getting everyone up for school; we were left to look after ourselves as kids.

I remember from a young age, my brothers had taken something from the shop, and I tried to cover it up; I remember telling my brothers to take the coke bottles to pay for the items. It turned out they were too late as the owner had spoken with parents, and when he found out, he was wild with rage. We got the razor strap and were hung up in hessian bags in the shed for a whole day as punishment.

This made me even more determined to be a stronger person. This strengthened my will and determination to not be pushed around or that I would allow people whom I cared for be abused.

My love for Food from a young age was nurtured by my great grandmother who was a great cook. She would make pastries that would go in one size and come out huge or making cakes.

She would have treats for us after school and let us lick the beaters, poor poppa. When I was young, visits to Nan's house was a way of escaping the abuse, so from a young age, helping her in the kitchen, my love of cooking evolved. I began work at the young age of 12 at KFC for independence.

When my stepfather left, mum remarried, I was 15 when I was kicked out of home, I lived on the streets until I found somewhere to live cheap, I would clean and cook as part of payment for the room in lieu of rent.

Putting myself through my last year of high school, where I finished school year 10, for schoolwork experience. I went to Sydney to work in a children's home for two weeks. It was my first adventure; I travelled on the train by myself to Coogee bay and spent a month working with kids not much younger than myself; I loved it. Matron offered me a job working with kids who were wards of the state.

I remember thinking about cooking and how it was my calling, so I returned back to my hometown to study Home Economics at TAFE; this was not easy as I was not very academic. I persevered as I would rather have fun travelling around on my motorbike.

So, when I had an opportunity to leave my hometown in Rural New South Wales aged 17 years old, I thought this was my chance to escape and be in charge of my destiny. I left on my motorbike to go on this adventure with my boyfriend; at the time, I had no job and a little bit of money in my pocket this was my ticket out of town.

When I arrived, I had to get work to survive, as it was expensive. I ended up working 3 jobs a cleaner sandwich shop kitchen hand at a resort in Alice Springs.

I put my hand up for the breakfast cook position, even though I didn't know what I was really getting myself into. I think I burnt about 20 loaves of bread, but I got through okay and was offered the apprenticeship in commercial cookery training under French and German chefs.

This was not easy as it was male, dominated industry, and there were not many female apprentices at the time when I was working; I remember at the time that it seemed odd but after starting my apprenticeship, I could see that it was very long hours for little pay and we would work weekends, public holidays and when the chef said you're on shift you would say yes chef turn up no questions asked, the chefs were incredibly old school and strict. I would leave my shifts upset and crying most nights but was determined to not show them they were getting to me.

Once I finished my apprenticeship, I would travel to gain

experiences, and I made a pledge to myself that I would not treat apprentices how I was treated. As a female chef, it was hard, you had to work twice as hard to get the positions for less pay. When I was younger my first executive chef position, the pay was less because I was a woman. I did the job and showed them my worth, but I was still not paid the same.

My career has spanned more than 40 plus years in this time, and I completed a Bachelor's degree in Education working in the education sector, working for TAFE, Le Cordon, Bleu, training nontrade / trade apprentices, commercial cookery, hospitality, the diversity in my learning and teaching of young chefs from a variety of cultures and nationalities.

My Chef's journey has allowed me to travel extensively through Australia, from working on a cruise ships many prestige's establishments, including 5-star restaurants, working through Europe and Asia. I've had the opportunity to work with lots of talented both female and male chefs and mentor young chefs.

Having worked as a TAFE teacher for 17 years, in this time, I was fortunate enough to teach a number of students. I got to travel in regional outback teaching on country to 1st nation students as well as apprentices trainees and showing them how amazing the hospitality in travel is; I taught a group of young indigenous women who were amazing, I was teaching these women and we were invited to cook in Dubbo for guidance where an amazing first Nations Chef Mark Olive was cooking. The students and I worked under his guidance at this event, preparing food etc., he was impressed with the women and asked if we would come and cook at the great escape in Western Australia.

When we went to Western Australia, we travelled to Margaret River, where we were invited to work with local schoolteachers, students from different areas of western Australia. We met at Margaret River, where we forage for a week and the students would attend a variety of masterclasses or making bread, pasta and milking cows to make ricotta. The students then prepared the foods with teachers & chefs. Students would showcase their dishes for lunch and cater for about 150 people. It was an amazing day and very life changing for these young students. Once the students completed their studies, they then set about on their own journey setting up their own catering businesses or working within the industry. This was a great outcome and I'm still proud of these women today and what they achieved.

Teaching and working in Papua New Guinea, I was able to teach young people the craft of cooking helping them to better their lives. One of the young girl apprentice chefs I taught in Papua New Guinea is still in contact with me still to this day, nearly 18 years; she has gone on to be the Head Chef / Manager in catering in Papua New Guinea.

Whilst working in South Australia, I was lucky enough to join the prestigious club for chef Les Toque Blanches at the young age of 24 years of age; to have the opportunity to work with various cultures and learning about different foods. This was such an honour as it proved to me that I had started to archive my dream of being a great chef and to be taken seriously.

Whilst being part of Les Torque Blanches would see me cooking for several charity events over many years to help raise monies for the Mary Potter Hospice, make a wish foundation, the great chefs of Adelaide luncheons. Having cooked for delegates, Sheiks, the Archbishop of Adelaide, and political leaders, Vocal artists and actors / Actresses.

I remember in 2011 receiving a call on my home number from an anonymous caller (at the time) to cater a VIP event and I would need to cater this VIP event; when I got off the phone I said to my husband (I thought it was a prank call) I need to do this catering job. It is big, but I cannot tell who it is and so my next thing was to convince fellow colleagues and people of my town to come and work on this exciting project but I'm unable to tell you what it is.

So this excitement grew in anticipation of who was coming, now remember I could have called on any chef friends to help with this event, and it would of elevated many a career in doing so.

I chose to keep the event community based where our town

could stand tall and empower the younger generation to think big and it does not matter where you come from; opportunities are always there for the taking, so I said to my husband I want to use my students and the local high school, so they can experience how amazing this industry really is and how it has changed my life.

So, I set about putting together a special lunch for (HRH) Princess Mary of Denmark with 280 of her closest friends as part of the royals given charity (RFDS). Royal flying doctors' Lunch was to be served in one of the hangers. We all started at 6 am in the morning of the event; we had to wait for RFDS mechanics to remove the planes from the hanger so that we could set up the tables and chairs etc., for the day, so with the help of nearly 70 volunteers, including local high school's students and young cookery & hospitality students as part of their final exam. I remember waiting for HRH to walk through to her seat; she made eye contact and said hello to each and every one of the students and volunteers on the day as she walked to her seat.

I was fortunate to meet HRH Princess Mary of Denmark out on the tarmac to present a dessert Assiette box, as she had to leave before the dessert was served. She was thanking me for a fabulous lunch; it was such an honour, and it was so good for the town. People are still talking about it. To this day, the students still come up to me in the street saying remember the lunch for HRH, watching them standing tall and have such pride about them.

I've had a successful career, having received many accolades, including the Award of Excellence for a 20-year contribution to the industry. Gold for the Adelaide Hills region for Australia in the Lifestyle Channel's 1999 Tasting Australia Regional Culinary Competition, one of the 10 great Chefs of Adelaide.

In 2016, I joined Chaîne des Rôtisseurs Association (Mondiale de la Gastronomies) with nearly 25,000 professional & amateur members, "a presence in more than "80 countries on 5 continents.

I was officially inducted in 2018 in the South Australia chapter (knighted); these clubs are very prestigious and well recognised in the industry. I've been part of the CWA as their cookery officer, and Volunteering and being part of the CWA community working alongside strong women who are community driven has been an amazing experience.

The Australian Culinary Federation is the "peak industry organisation representing professional Chefs, Cooks, Young Chefs, Apprentices and Culinary Students.

In 2011, I started my own food product utilising Bush Foods (Pandora's Palate Bush Flavours) was born, in a variety of items from Chutneys jam salts and to sauces & a side order of catering business in people's homes, weddings, events, and the business grew substantially.

So, at the end of 2019, I decided to leave my full-time position to concentrate on my own business. We just started catering for the Indian Pacific doing their off-train experiences when Covid hit in March 2020. We then had to stop Catering and re-evaluate what this meant in the New World — so using this time to pivot ourselves as we are unable to cater to the public. We then started to cater for film crew's where we operated for six months during Covid on the MINISERIES, the Royal Flying Doctors. Fast forward to 2021, we would start to operate to the public again after the first closure for Covid.

What it has shown us is we needed a kitchen, our own forever home so we were on the lookout; when we found our forever home and the negotiations started in January 2021, and on May 27th, 2021, we received the keys to our Building, which is an old heritage, listed building built in 1888, would need a lot of renovations.

Covid hit again, and we had six months in lockdown, there was no work for staff, but everybody was on board to wait out for what was to come. My husband, and I started about cleaning, renovating the space that we had to then open; we replaced pretty much everything after nearly 20 plus years of neglect. We replaced the Kitchen and gutted the dining room 6 months later; we opened the doors Jan 2022 and never looked back so the old saltbush was born. The word is spreading far and wide, to open a restaurant has been a dream for many years; when I had my catering business, we would go to people's homes and facilitate private fine dining dinners in their homes. I open a restaurant that can welcome people as if I'm working in them to my home and The Old Saltbush Restaurant and Catering, a retro style of quality dining experience mixed with old-fashioned hospitality was created.

"I wanted to create something unique for our regional town in the far west, for people go away and go to nice fancy restaurants and say, 'they we went away, it was so lovely', I wanted that here. Because at the end of the day, we deserve that something special in Broken Hill, we're not hillbillies; we deserve the good things in life as well." Offering a menu that is part ode to the pastoral industry and part bush experience in the use of saltbush, the restaurant is indeed a gem. And the word is spreading far and wide.

Since opening the restaurant, we have received a few accolades for best new business, best excellence in hospitality and tourism and the big one, the outback spirit award, which is testimony to how we run our business and that we need to lift each other up and support one another in our endeavours.

Where to now?

Over the course of more than 40 years of teaching and training, helping many young people achieve their dreams to mentoring many chefs who are now high-profile in their own right have a couple that come to mind. One is one of the young apprentices who started with me when I was 16 now 38, and when he was married, I went to his wedding, his children, both still young, they are still very much part of my life. He rings me often to check in and it's always Chef how's things and we chat, which is nice. Another young chef, who started with me when he was 16, emailed me about 12- 15 years ago now saying thank you for being his chef and how the training etc., had helped him and he was appreciative and mentioned that it took 10 years to realise what he learnt, now that he was training his own apprentices.

My vision and impact in the hospitality industry is to support each other by lifting each other up, celebrate our wins together and grow the pie. This can be done through buying locally and utilising what's in your own backyard; metaphorically speaking, we community minded so that we can all be self-reliant. I'm growing my pie by supporting other local businesses in my community, employing people from a variety of ages and cultures, and telling the story through Food.

It's been a long hard journey with its ups and downs in life. Whatever you wanna call it, yes it is hard trying to make your mark working in a male-dominated industry, If anything, it has taught me resilience, determination, not to / don't give up, to be humble, and take it in your stride.

What I've learnt from on my life journey so far is don't give up, you keep your eye on the prize and just go for it; give it a crack because it's your dream, and nobody can take those away from you. If I saw my younger self on the street, I would say don't give up; you're on the right track work hard, play hard and listen to your heart, and you will achieve great things.

We need to grow the pie in the community and to support each other's wins and help each other when we fall down. If anything, Yes, it's hard, it's not easy; we don't always get what we want but if we continue and stay true to what we want, it will happen.

Culinary regards, Chef

About the Author

Lee Cecchin is the founder/owner of The Old Salt Bush Restaurant & Catering. Born in Australia, now residing in New South Wales, Australia, and is an International Chef/Restauranteur. From humble beginnings, Lee has built a prestigious career in the hospitality Industry as a Chef for more than 40 years. Lee has cooked for royalty such as HRH Princess Mary of Denmark, Sheiks, political leaders worked on film sets catering for various actors, actresses and has travelled worked extensively through Australia, Europe and Asia.

Chef Cecchin has accumulated prestigious awards and is a member of the highly acclaimed la Chaîne des Rôtisseurs, Les Toque Blanches clubs. While living far west regional outback town Chef Lee has her own line of award-winning food products produced using locally/regionally sourced ingredients including using bush foods giving unique flavour. Lee loves to travel and socialise with friends for her favourite coffee at local coffee shop.

Email: hello@theoldsaltbush.com.au
Facebook: www.facebook.com/theoldsaltbush
Website: www.theoldsaltbush.com.au

Natasha Coughlan

"The future belongs to those who believe in the beauty of their dreams."

I'm one of the luckiest woman alive.

Wait a second.

Is it luck or something else?

Well, to get the answer, let's read on.

My name is Natasha. I am a mum, a wife, and an entrepreneur. I have created a life that people dream of, an amazing husband who is supportive of all of my ambitions. We have 3 amazing, beautiful boys who are smart, healthy, and amazing global citizens of the world. I live in one of the most beautiful places in Australia and I'm so grateful to have been able to travel the world with my husband and my three boys. I have an Empire of businesses, and I help other women just like you create amazing lives by design.

My life though could have gone either way, I was born in 1981 in a small country town of around 10,000 people. My mother who was a child herself, only 17 years old, thanks to her determination, delinquency, and total disregard to please people by following the rules here I am. I was a really good kid, a kind kid, one thing I always knew was my mum lived for me. I look back as an adult, a mum, and a wife, and can see that she struggled with her own identity and insecurities, and she searched my whole childhood for unconditional love. My grandmother, and her mother, Joyce didn't want my mum to have me and told her to "get rid of it." Joyce would often tell me I ruined my mum's life, that I shouldn't be here, that I should be more like my older cousin, and often said that I was a horrible child. I was always the spunky kid, the one that was always the one in trouble. My elder cousin was the golden child, and my grandmother Joyce wanted me to be more like him. His stepdad molested me when I was roughly 5 a few times while my mum was working nights and I was staying at my auntie's.

My mum had a boyfriend from when I was two, he owned the pub that she worked at when I was six we moved with her boyfriend to the big smoke. He was a property developer and had a few projects going on there. I was excited to leave everything in this small town behind, knowing, even at the age of six, that this would be a massive benefit in my life. The only thing I was sad about was leaving my best friend that I had had for as long as I could remember.

My childhood was anything but stable. We moved a lot and

sometimes with no warning or planning, my mum and her boyfriend had a very tumultuous relationship, they would break up, get back together, and do it all over again. I remember laying in bed a lot and just hearing them fight, argue and yell at one another. This one night I remember mum waking me in the middle of the night, putting me in my dressing gown, ushering me into the car, and telling me we were going for a drive. We went around to lots of places that I knew; her boyfriend's office, friends' house, the local pub, and finally my mum's best friend's house, and that's where he was. The next day we were packed up, bird and all, we headed off, back to my auntie's in the small country town.

I was never really able to make any real friends throughout primary school and early high school, we moved so much, 9 schools, and I was teased constantly. I have a smile that shows a little more of my top gum and got the nickname gummy bear. This nickname followed me for a long time.

In high school, after we moved back to the big smoke alone, me and my mum, I went to a pretty rough school. I was endlessly bullied, beaten up, and harassed, I was about 15 and I became a bit of a recluse. I was scared to leave my house in case I was going to be beaten up. I thought of ending my life a few times. I was very lonely and depressed. When I did tell the teachers and counsellors at school, their response was "they're just jealous of you".

The only reason that I didn't take my own life was that my mum and I were on our own, it was just her and I, she was happy, I could never imagine leaving her on her own after everything that she'd done for me, despite my grandmother's words, "your mum would be better off without you." Then her boyfriend was back, and back in we moved. So our house wasn't happy a lot of the time, there was tension and friction, fighting and arguing, when I was 17, my stepdad and I had a big fight and I was kicked out of the house.

I remember packing my little green mini with all my clothes, my school things, and my sound system, and remember backing out of the driveway while my mum stood there crying, we've always been extremely close, so this was sad for both of us. I had never felt this lonely in my life.

I was in my second last year of high school. I had to get two jobs at 5:00 AM: a breakfast shift -head to school then go to work at a bar. I found school difficult with undiagnosed dyslexia and learning difficulties, I was just put in the column of naughty and disruptive.

My boyfriend of nearly two years cheated on me, my best friend of years stopped talking to me. I was drinking a lot, I was street racing and looking for somebody to approve, love, and like me.

I got a job in Sydney, so I packed up my car, rented a room, and moved. Sydney was not any different, I got into recreational drugs, I drank a lot, still looking for somebody to love me.

I was in a relationship at the time and I found myself stalking my boyfriend. This had been happening with all my boyfriends I just wasn't aware of.

We headed overseas together, didn't last very long, we broke up and I flew home to where my mom was living. I wasn't allowed to live in my mom's house as her boyfriend and I still didn't see eye to eye.

I was working in nightclubs and bars. I got hooked on prescription weight-loss drugs whilst drinking and spent my life partying. I found myself at parties held by Bikie gangs, and hanging out with drug dealers and in a lot of situations that could have been extremely dangerous.

I was still looking for somebody to love me. I was still looking outside of myself for acceptance. I didn't realize at the time that there's only one person that can create your happiness, and your self-worth and that is you. At one stage I was homeless, I was sleeping on people's couches, I even slept in my car.

At 24 I met my first husband, I moved interstate for him to do a trade and we lived underneath his parent's house. I worked hard to support us while he was doing his apprenticeship. I would stand at the door and listen to him and his mother talking upstairs about how I was no good for him and that he could do much better. His mum also declared she wasn't coming to our wedding or supporting our marriage. I felt unwanted, unloved, and unworthy. When he left me, I decided that I was worth more. I moved up to where my mom was, who by the way is now a lesbian, happier than ever, and has an amazing partner, my stepmom Kim. I sat down and I made a list of the person that I wanted to be, I didn't want to let my past dictate who I was or who I was going to be.

I created a list of my attributes and thought about how I had been sabotaging my relationships based on what had happened in my childhood. I made a commitment to myself that I deserve a life where I'm happy, loved, wanted, and cherished.

I sat down and created a checklist of my perfect man. Soon after I made this list came along my now amazing husband Zane, he turned up extremely quickly after I had put my list together and out into the universe. I was still traumatised from my previous relationship, so we took it extremely slow but I was still scared that it was too good to be true or that he was an axe murderer. My mum said to go for it, don't brush him off, you deserve a guy just like him... I look back now and I may have been self-sabotaging my happiness because I still subconsciously didn't think I deserved it. I had never in my life felt unconditional love from a partner and I am so glad I didn't settle for less.

And here I sit at my favourite coffee shop overlooking the ocean, it is 30 degrees Celsius with 81% humidity and with a 70% chance of rain so my hair is going crazy. I think about the life that I have designed, crafted, and chosen. Every choice I make these days is on purpose, thought about and I'm present for every single choice. I first ask myself will this serve me, is this something that will help me go towards my goals and be a better person and a better version of myself or is it not?

I think about how hard this process has been. This whole writing of my story has been extremely hard. My mentor once said to me "You need to get comfortable with telling your story, you are being selfish by not sharing it to help others." He also taught me about living in obligation, the obligation to help as many people as I can, an obligation to those who need me to do the best I can, my kids, my husband, my family, my friends, my teams and the people that I will help that I don't even know yet.

When I first tried sharing my story, I was so self-conscious even though I thought I had accepted everything that had happened to me in my life, it was extremely hard to believe that my story, experiences and achievements would benefit anyone. I subconsciously said to my coach one day "What do I have to offer people, I mean what would anyone gain from me?"

I got the kick in the butt I needed that day from my coach and myself. Being able to see when we are self-sabotaging is a major step. Being aware makes the process so much easier to change and choose a different option, my coach helped me this day. He pointed out how amazing I am, what I had achieved and accomplished in the six short months that we had been together. He said "you just get shit done" my amazing life is proof of that, he also said to me "If I hear that from you again..." I didn't need him to finish the sentence as I knew that nothing good or productive was coming from this limiting belief. It's funny just when I think I've got to a point where I don't need any more coaching or mentoring, bam, something else hits me.

I have accepted now that having coaches and mentors is lifelong. Because at different stages you need different advice. Surrounding myself with like-minded people that lift me is key to continual growth and improvement. I spend my days doing what I want, unapologetically. I used to feel bad having my own time and doing things for myself that didn't involve my husband or my kids or weren't for them. Now I realise that being the best version of myself is the best for everyone, giving myself time out to re-calibrate, rest and recover helps everybody. Being congruent in myself is something that is of utmost importance to me. your actions need to be those of where you want your life to be, so your wants and dreams paired with the actions needed to achieve these is being congruent.

If you are congruent you are a better mom, a happier person, and a better friend. Being true to yourself and your wants and needs and desires does a few things, it helps you distinguish people, activities, actions, and thoughts that don't serve you, or get you closer to your goals. For example, I always wanted to be a stay-at-home mom, I wanted to spend as much time with my kids as I could.

I chose to have them and didn't want to send them off for somebody else to raise. My husband and I got an opportunity after putting it out into the universe to relocate to Indonesia as expats for his work. It was a great opportunity. The package was amazing and included vacations, schooling, housing, and the best part I didn't have to work and was able to be at home with our kids.

I have always felt a huge desire for more, knowing that I didn't want to be mediocre, I didn't want to follow the rules and I didn't want to work for someone else. When we returned to Australia, all my children were back at school. I was a little lost, I felt like I had no purpose anymore and had to find something for myself. We struggled to relocate back to Australia financially, so I went out and I got myself a job. I had always felt guilty that my husband was the main income earner, but I did understand that our kids benefited from me being at home, picking them up from school, dropping them off, and sending the kids and my husband cooked lunch each day. I loved that time of my life and I'm so grateful that we had the opportunity to do so.

So I got a job at a school that wasn't congruent with my values, I left before the kids went to school, I got home after them and to be quite honest with you I hated working for someone else, I know myself and I know I was made to be something more- to create, change, and impact people's lives.

I know my personality type, and I know what I want out of my life. I know that I want to impact as many people as I can, and I didn't feel congruent with what I was doing and what I wanted in my life. Some people don't think that the stress of building companies, putting out fires, mentoring staff, building teams, creating products, and negotiating is exciting. All this stuff excites me to no end.

The point is knowing what I want in my life and having a clear visual of my goals and what I want to do, be, and have created opportunities and clear pathways to achieve.

At this point in my life, I have a meditation practice including affirmations, an exercise and eating WOL and always listening to great books.

The most crucial part of my success in business and life is having a mentor and coach.

So I became one!

I love helping people find their self-worth, and learn to love themselves. One girl in particular, had major depression, she was bullied terribly at school, had a very shitty home life, and was very overweight, and had thought that everyone in her life would be better off if she wasn't around. We worked on building her up, believing in herself, and loving herself. She is now married to a great guy that loves each and every part of her. Life has never been better.

Being able to help women create businesses and property portfolios to give them not only income but feel empowered is amazing, and they can arrange it around their life.

Helping people is something I am passionate about and would love to help you with sharing my free e-book, 'How to be unapologetically happy." You can download it over on my website www.natashacoughlan.com

Having your own income and purpose is so empowering, creating something that you truly believe in is uplifting. Being able to spend time with your family and your friends without restrictions that's empowerment.

I'm also privileged to be heading over to Cambodia with my family to do some volunteer work in the middle of the year, building houses and digging trenches for water supply to villages. I can only do this because I have created a life by design.

This year I am so pumped to help as many women as I can create a life they love, want, and can be proud of. I am thrilled to have two speaking events already this year and many more to come. I believe that speaking events, including podcasts and live events, are the most effective way to reach as many women as I can. I am offering more of my time for one on one coaching to help women find their power and inspiration and feel more confident to create the life they want and deserve.

I've always dreamed of writing a book, it's been on my vision board forever, along with women supporting women and I'm so grateful that I had this opportunity to be part of this project. Keep up to date with what I'm doing and I would also love to get a message from you if you found my story helpful or share with me what action or commitment you've taken since reading my story to create a life by your design.

So to the amazing beautiful, strong woman reading this, I am so proud to be able to share part of my story with you, my only wish is that you can take something, even just one thing that I've mentioned in this book, and use it to create your life by design.

About the Author

Natasha Coughlan is an award-winning Australian Entrepreneur and Speaker. Living on the Sunshine Coast, Queensland, Australia, Natasha has built an empire of businesses and helps others to do the same by sharing her story and experience on global platforms, empowering women across the globe via speaking and private coaching to create a life by design unapologetically.

In her first year in business, Natasha was a finalist in the AusMumpreneur awards and the Australian Women's Small Business awards. Natasha is an award-winning property investor. Natasha is the mum of 3 boys and loves spending family time watching them play rugby, she also enjoys camping and traveling. Natasha spends a lot of time working on herself professionally and personally, she believes that growth in both areas keeps you at the top of your game.

Email: Admin@natashacoughlan.com
Website: www.natashacoughlan.com
Facebook: www.facebook.com/natashacoughlan1

Karen Dawn

I have a tattoo on my left foot: "What Doesn't Kill You Makes You Stronger. "

This has been the story of my Life so far!

Thank goodness for positivity, resourcefulness, inner strength I never even knew I had, and a wicked sense of humour for the times that nothing else made sense!

Life should have been different, My Parents divorced when I was 4. We embarked on a twisted journey of emotional divorce tactics, hatred back & forth, vicious custody battles using the children as pawns – subconsciously and consciously.

I was kidnapped when I was 5, and had men break into my bedroom when I was 7.

I was scarred mentally and emotionally; I was terrified of the dark. I would hear any small noise at night, and I would lay awake listening for hours.

The emotional, verbal and manipulative battle between my parents kept going for years.

Eventually, as an adult I told them both to stop their shit! What happened between them was none of my business & it should have stayed that way!

I didn't realise it yet, but I was repeating the generational pattern I was raised with.

I met my ex-husband at age 17, that is the way I thought things were supposed to happen….. you meet someone and move in together and start making a future. White picket fences & little house on the prairie style!

We were married in 1988, and his "bucks party" was in the backyard of my "hens party" so he could keep an eye on everything. I was too young & too naive to know about coercive control or red flags back then.

He cheated and lied so many times. I felt broken, betrayed, and hurt beyond measure. I begged him to stay that I would fix things, I would let him do whatever he wanted, just please don't go!

Hindsight is a wonderful thing! If I knew back then, what I know now, I would have packed his bags for him. I was too co-dependent and had such low self-esteem & low self-worth.

I was almost 30 before I gave birth to my first Beautiful Daughter & experienced the joy of being a Mum. My 2nd Gorgeous daughter was born in 2000.

He complained that we didn't have enough money for me to stay home. So when my 2nd born was 6 months old, I started doing party plan – women's clothes & lingerie.

I was super surprised to find myself breaking sales records, winning prizes, earning money and best of all, my confidence was blossoming.

I was a natural, I loved helping women, I loved seeing other women happy. I started teaching other women how to run their own business, and they started to feel the same as I did.

I won 4 overseas holidays, unfortunately I was not "allowed" to take them.

I was flown all expenses paid to Sales Conventions & Speaking in front of hundreds of women, inspiring them to believe in themselves & achieve their goals and dreams.

I ran my business while pregnant with my 3rd amazing daughter and took all 3 girls with me to as many meetings and conferences as I could.

OH MY GOSH!!! It was a complete surprise to be presented with the first ever Company Car and a 21 Diamond ring for the Company 21st Year Celebrations.

I was a Successful Business Woman, I was a Mumpreneur!

My ultimate joy was seeing the lightbulb of happiness in another woman's eyes that I had helped to inspire – just doing what I loved doing!

My heart was Full!

He still wasn't happy! I was earning more money than he was! He was sick of looking after the children while I worked! Why didn't I give him a son, he yelled at me for being a failure as a child bearer too!

That was the pattern I had become used to, whenever I was happy & felt good about myself, he would set about to demolish my confidence & self-esteem. He was not happy until I was in tears, broken on the floor. Each time it would take me days to recover emotionally & mentally.

He gave me an ultimatum – My Business or my Marriage. I regret making the wrong decision.

He had started working in the mines, away from home. Quite frankly, I was relieved, I didn't need him around the house, I could do it by myself & if I didn't know how, I would learn.

Most importantly, we had 3 happy, healthy daughters. Still not enough Karen!

I was never allowed to see his phone, his bank accounts, or look in his wallet. He had always kept secrets, porn under his car seats or blatantly in the house.

When I found out about his next affair, after all I had given up for him, for our marriage, I was shattered – 110% broken.

We needed a clean start. So we would rent out our home & move out to Blackwater to live as a family in the mining town so we could all be together.

Stupid Woman!! Everything got worse!

He would get angry & swear at the children for taking too long closing the gate, checking the mail, and putting their bikes away. Pretty much anything!

He would get angry at me for taking too long at the grocery store, for not being home when he got home from work, or for having "coffee" with friends.

If I dared to ask to go to a work BBQ, or Safety Award Recognition at the Mining Camp, with my Supervisors & Crew he would explode and threaten all sorts of violent repercussions.

I was simply not "allowed" to be a happy wife, mother or woman.

I became so hypervigilant, I would watch every little thing the girls did, so that I could hurry them up or pull them up before he did, but nothing I did was ever enough.

One night his temper was out of control, he smashed a glass & held it to my throat.

My 3 Beautiful daughters were watching out their bedroom window…… That was the moment I knew this had to end!

"If you lock that fucking door, I will fucking kill you. And if you call the police it will be the last thing you ever fucking do!"

The 4 of us sat with our backs against the bathroom door, hugging each other crying & shaking uncontrollably. Courthouse visits, urgent DVO's and Crisis Housing came next.

I remember one of my daughters saying "I wish he actually hit you Mum, so the police would just believe us"

I had finally found the strength to leave the prison of our existence - and then all hell broke loose. My 3 daughters were innocent souls caught up in the whirlwind of chaos.

I worked full-time & sent the children to before & after-school care, the rent in mining towns is ridiculously high.

He would not agree to any formal parenting orders, and demanded 50/50 care to begin with, this was so challenging & harmful for the children. He would constantly threaten to keep them, tell them that they would never see Mummy again.

I had to supply everything for the girls, including pillows & toothbrushes. He would wake my 11-year-old up at 5am when he went to work for 12-hour shifts, and it was up to her to get her younger sisters ready for school and walk them there as well. My baby girl had to grow up way too fast & become a mother to her sisters while I was not there. He didn't know how to be a caring Father, he only knew "his way or the highway."

It soon became evident that we were never loved, we were just possessions. My Trauma Counsellor opened my eyes to what a textbook Narcissist was, and he absolutely ticked every box.

For the next 2 years, we endured endless verbal abuse, stalking, and violent threats.

It became a living hell trying to stay in close vicinity, and eventually, the local Blackwater police & my solicitor advised us to move 45 minutes further west to Emerald, as they could not guarantee our safety any longer. When he found out, he erupted in a vile tantrum of rage.

He told the girls that they had 24 hours to get their belongings, or he was taking it all to the dump. I honestly could not see how any man could sink much lower, but he proved me wrong.

He quit his full-time mining job so he didn't have to pay child support and moved 6 hours away from his daughters. The 4 of us struggled to make ends meet – but we did it!

Until 4pm New Year's Eve 2011, when our lives did a complete 360. I was 43 years old when I was almost killed in a reckless vehicle "incident"; this was not an accident.

My boyfriend was close to finalising custody with his ex-wife. We had arranged to meet her in a park in Theodore, the boys ran back to their Mum exchanging Xmas presents & hugs. Then she started loading the boys into the back seat of her elderly father's 4wd.

We ran over, my boyfriend grabbed the keys out of the ignition, and he climbed into the backseat to release his sons from their seat belts. The boys were upset & crying, everyone was yelling, and my 3 daughters were watching as it all unfolded.

I saw the old man grab a 2nd set of keys & put them in the ignition. I instinctively put my hand through the window to grab the keys too.

Everything happened so quickly, he grabbed my arm & pulled me further through the driver's window. My eldest daughter stood in front of the bull bar & I saw my other girls holding each other on the grass crying & scared. He held onto my arm through the steering wheel while he started the car & started driving.

I tried to keep up, I was running, then side hopping, then I lost my footing altogether.

He only let go of my arm when he needed to change to 2nd gear. I fell backwards & hit my head on the open rear passenger door and smashed down head over heels 7 or 8 times on the bitumen until I landed in the middle of the road unconscious & bleeding.

The Royal Flying Doctors airlifted me to Brisbane. I spent 3 days on Life support, followed by a week in a coma. My whole world had turned upside down & the emotions were crashing in on me. Highly medicated I was trying to fathom what had happened, I was inundated with pain, the ringing in my head & intense pressure felt like it was about to explode.

I couldn't think straight, I couldn't talk properly, I couldn't move properly, I didn't know if I was going to live or die.

One week after coming out of the coma, I was discharged by the hospital, by myself, in Brisbane with my bag in one hand & drugs in the other. I was not given any information about rehabilitation and felt so lost and alone.

I don't remember much of the next week, except the joy & sheer relief of seeing my children again. They were my reason; they were the only thing that kept me fighting to survive, fighting to Live.

Apparently, I had fallen through the cracks of the public health system, but I was so thankful to be alive. I started to learn more about my injuries.

I had sustained traumatic brain injury, with a fracture to the base of my skull & 3 haematomas to the left side of my skull, a fractured left ear canal, several lacerations to my head, inside my mouth, on my forehead & right between my eyes. I had blurry vision and lots of missing memories.

I could barely hear at all, my ears were ringing non-stop, my speech was affected & my words were slurred, I had anosmia a total loss of taste & smell, constant fatigue & chronic pain, dizziness & balance problems.

The next 11 months were a rollercoaster of emotions, physical & mental rehabilitation.

The relationship had dissolved & the girls and I went into crisis housing in Emerald.

I was now on a disability pension with zero child support & on the housing commission list. We had to focus on the positives – together, we had "girl power" The girls were amazing; they helped every day to do the chores that were near impossible for me.

I started researching more about Brain Injury & I found an online support group on Facebook.

I also began a legal claim against the people responsible for almost killing me & leaving me with lasting injuries that had affected my Life, and my children's lives forever. It was a 3rd party Injury insurance claim, as absolutely NO police charges were laid against the old man. In fact, I was actually warned off laying any charges, as he was an elder with the Brethren church in Chinchilla.

PTSD hit me hard with a double whammy onslaught 13 months after my injuries. Sometimes during a panic attack, I would black out, and not remember anything that happened. The girls learnt how to help calm me down & I learnt techniques to minimise the triggers as much as I could.

My insurance claim was eventually successful, so in 2014, we moved back to the Coast to keep healing & recovering. We found a low set 4-bedroom brick home in Yeppoon that had a big yard for the girls, bushland at the back for privacy, on the top of a quiet cul-de-sac for safety, within walking distance to schools & shops. Finally, we had a place of our own to call HOME!

I had always been super resourceful & organised. Google had become my best friend & I made lots of new online friends. My confidence was re-emerging, I was rediscovering my Self Worth & my inner Happiness.

Almost losing my Life & having to relearn lots of skills gave me the Freedom to become my Authentic genuine self, after so many years of living in hypervigilance and fear.

This was a powerful positive to come from so many negatives, that same positivity started to light my fire. It became the wind beneath my wings.

I had reached a point in my rehabilitation & healing that I now had to accept how to live with the ongoing issues that could not scientifically improve any further.

I had been researching a lot about Nutrition & Natural supplements to help with my own Mental Health, Brain fog, Energy, Sleep, Weight loss and hormonal changes.

I aligned with a Leading Network Marketing Company & started reigniting my skills from before my injuries, as well as gaining new skills. I loved it and soon started to build a successful business again.

As a solo parent, I made a lot of mistakes, but I was a damn good Mum. It was not easy making decisions on my own or having to stand my ground. Nothing was the same as when I grew up.

I looked for resources, I used Parentline Counselling services, and I searched the Internet for advice & solutions to issues my teens were going through. There was plenty of information on babies, toddlers, and young children, but there was not much support for raising teens.

So I became the proud Founder of Mum's Parenting Teens Australia Facebook Group!

Now with the help of some amazing women who volunteer their time to keep the group a safe haven for all our Mums, we have built that group to over 15,000 members.

As my Beautiful Daughters grew through that hormonal teenager phase, I gained so much strength from having a virtual support network.

I started to feel myself being pulled toward a higher reason for my survival, but what was it?

During my recovery, I did a lot of counselling & Self Development to learn how to live again - I had rediscovered my authentic self & regained my confidence.

I strongly feel that even the most painful events and disappointments can hold the potential and promise for greatness and fulfilment if we learn from them.

That is what I wanted to start sharing with others.

As I reflected on where I came from, what I went through, and how I had triumphed, rising time & time again like a Phoenix from the ashes. I realised that was my purpose!

Everything in my Life has led me to this revelation. Every aspect of my predestined Life had changed completely after I turned 40.

Perfectly Imperfect Women 40+ Community was born!

I have endured & survived more than many women, but not as much abuse & trauma as other warriors. I have hit rock bottom – emotionally, physically, mentally & I have clawed my way back.

I have used my resourcefulness, my intelligence, my heart centred personality, and endless positivity to reclaim my power & passion. I have transformed my Life from Victim to Victorious!

I am here to help other Women recognise that they are Perfect just the way they are, they are Good Enough, they are Worthy, and they are undeniably creatures of untold resilience & unlimited potential.

I provide Connection, Conversations, Practiced Methods & Recommendations to evolve & change into who you want to become, not just who society, family members or past generations think you should become.

Women want to be Accepted for who they are, Celebrated for everything they do for others and Loved unconditionally just the way they are – Perfectly Imperfect. ♥

I relate to you, because I have been you, I meet you where you are, because I have been there too!

Do you want to feel more Positive, Confident, Empowered, Passionate & Resourceful?

I truly welcome you to my story & to our Community of Perfectly Imperfect Women. ♥

About the Author

Karen Dawn has risen from the darkness of despair and overcome traumatic upheaval in her Life over & over again, to now be recognised as an Inspirational Beacon of Positivity, Resilience & Recovery to Tens of Thousands of people in her online Support Groups. Karen Dawn is the Founder & CEO of Mum's Parenting Teens Australia and Perfectly Imperfect Women 40+. She is also a successful Elite Online Business Coach teaching Digital Attraction Marketing, Relationship Building and Global Networking. Her goal is to Impact over 1 million Families & enable them to create an extra income while sharing high quality, effective products in the online space.

Karen knows you are NOT "just" a Mother, "just" a Wife or "just" an ordinary Woman. She knows YOU are the Whole Incredible Package – a Truly Beautiful, Magnificent inside & out, Perfectly Imperfect Woman!! We are all here to help each other SHINE.

Website: https://connect.karendawn.org
Facebook: www.facebook.com/karenbowengiles
Group: www.facebook.com/groups/perfectlyimperfectwomen

Melissa Haggarty

Allow Life to be Magical

Does life feel hard? Are you questioning how you became so lost? Are you feeling alone, anxious, exhausted, unseen, rejected and abandoned? Do you ache to stand up and say, "FUCK THIS"?

Would you like to feel confident, vibrant, supported and in control of creating your future?

It is time to choose you. Choose to follow that spark flickering inside you. It is your soul trying to get your attention to let you know you are off track and life is meant to be better than what you are experiencing right now.

I am here to help you use your courage and strength to reconnect with your soul, release your self-limiting patterns and ignite your inner warrior to unleash your infinite possibilities. It is time for you to live in your power and freedom and create the life you desire.

In simple terms, we exist as two main parts. Our human self and our soul self. To make it clearer to separate the two, I separate my human self as my logical mind, the part that thinks, and my soul self as the part that feels. When we are living disconnected from our soul, we are very much in our head and make decisions using our logic and ego rather than our intuition and gut instinct.

I invite you to do the following simple exercise to experience the difference between the human and the soul self.

1. Identify a decision you need to make.

2. Identify all the options you have about this decision and write each option on a separate sticky note.

3. Place the sticky notes on the floor with space in between each note.

4. Now choose a single sticky note (option) and stand on this sticky note.

5. Close your eyes and breathe until you feel calm.

6. Draw your attention to your mind and ask your mind what it thinks about this option.

7. Now draw your attention to where you feel your centre is. This may be your heart, stomach, or up in the stars. Ask your soul how it feels about this option.

Can you feel the difference between your human self and soul self? Sometimes the two selves are not aligned, and you need to honour both selves and compromise until you find yourself in a place where both selves are aligned.

I haven't always helped others in this way, and for many years I worked as an industrial chemist in commissioning and managerial roles in the resources energy sector. I went to university, got a degree, and got a job in the field of my degree. I was following what I believed was the norm and what was expected of me. I was successful in this career and continued to achieve in each new job opportunity.

However, inside my being and in my relationships, a very different story was playing out.

In my twenties, I would greet each day by pulling back the curtains, saying "Hello World". Life was full of possibilities and I achieved anything I wanted. I felt vibrant, successful, on track and positive.

In my early thirties, I was searching for more and couldn't grasp what it was I was looking for. My marriage was falling apart. I was focused on work, paying off a mortgage and stuck in a routine. Life became mediocre, boring and predictable. Life was starting to disappoint me.

My marriage ended, and I shoved down my emotions and got

on with it. Off I went to work and kept myself busy. I had life decisions to make, like choosing where to live and sorting out my divorce and finances. I made all my decisions from my logical mind.

I experienced other romantic relationships. As these progressed, I began to feel alone, deep agony, despair, rejected and confused on the inside. I realised that my life was full of emotionally unavailable relationships. This pattern showed up in romantic partnerships, parental relationships and work relationships. I blamed others for their shortcomings and inability to love me as I desired to be loved. I was a people pleaser, going along with things and tolerating my discomfort to make others happy. I believed I had to please others to be loved by them. I was disconnected from my soul, and I looked to others for love and validation. I trusted others too early, and I was Miss Fix It trying to fix others. I was walled up in self-protection to protect myself from rejection and abandonment. I was emotionally unavailable. The walls around my heart felt heavy and rock solid. I was aching to be seen and heard. I was powerless.

Conversations with others with the intent of resolving issues were bamboozling. I'd start a conversation and the other person would somehow end up accusing me or blaming me for the very thing I was trying to address with them. Issues were never resolved and were buried creating an ever-growing, festering mess.

Fast forward to my forties, and I was fed up, exhausted and confused. Another romantic relationship I deeply desired to work out began to unravel, triggering my deepest wounds of rejection and abandonment. I began to question why was this happening again. An inner spark in me flickered and I believed somewhere deep inside that life was meant to be better than this. My soul whispered, "STOP". And I did. I simply stopped.

It felt like I had skidded up against a solid line that could not be crossed without understanding how I had arrived at this position. At that moment, it felt like all I could do was say, "Fuck This". I'd had a gutful and vowed I would do whatever was required to cross the line and get myself out of where I was. The next clear message I received was, "You are the common denominator in your experiences". This hit with brutal force and I felt winded like I'd been punched in the guts. I exhaled a slow, "Fuuuuuccccccckkkkk".

I began my journey of owning my bullshit since I was the common denominator in all my experiences. I went on retreats, joined online programs and dived into all things related to our soulful self and how our unconscious mind drives so much of our behaviour.

I started observing how I was playing in life from a raw, honest place. I recognised I was fed up with the repeating patterns that were depleting my energy. It felt like swallowing a bunch of bitter pills that scraped and burned on the way down. I choked, raged and cried through owning my bullshit. I had many defining moments where I saw the truth of my reality and my part in each situation. It was my deep knowing that helped me see my truth and also my deep knowing that prevented me from unseeing what I was learning. My desire to move from where I was to the other side of the line pulled me forward. I reconnected with my soul and allowed all the emotions to surface and release. I forgave myself for tolerating other people's bullshit and thinking it was my job to fix them. In parental and work relationships I also simply let go. I realised my soul had always been trying to get my attention and I was the one who had been ignoring the messages.

On the practical side of life, I strongly desired a break from full-time work and I recognised I was burnt out. I needed time out from all areas of life. I had no final destination in mind, just pure freedom, to choose what I wanted to do and when. It was all about the journey.

I chose myself and leaped. I resigned from my job. I had to overcome limiting self-beliefs to leave my job as I was raised to appreciate my job and not take it for granted and I felt I was just throwing it away. The only time I'd ever resigned from a job was to commence a new job. It was a pull between my soulful self, calling me to let go and my human self, worried about how I was going to live. Before resigning, I looked at my finances to determine how long I could cover expenses without an income.

My employer asked if there was anything they could do to retain me. I requested extended leave and they agreed to hold my job for twelve months. The safety net of holding my job was my compromise to find a balance between my human self and soul self. A Mazda Bongo minivan appeared for sale after a couple of weeks of resigning. It fell in my lap as the Bongo was located only twenty minutes from my home. I became a solo woman travelling in her Bongo van. I sank into the earth, I explored, I raged, I cursed, I dreamed, I released, I opened. I had expectations for each journey and my soul always taught me something far greater that I needed to know.

I went through a period of feeling isolated without work interaction. Old friendships reawakened and new friendships appeared. Opportunities in all areas of life appeared. I learned to let go of expectations and attachments to outcomes. Often things didn't make sense to my logical mind, and I learned the correct path was always revealed when I followed my gut. I am so grateful I took the leap into the unknown and gave myself the space to come home to me. I was free.

I realised those closest to us are like a mirror reflecting to us, our own beliefs and behaviours we need to acknowledge and release. Life became simple. I experienced that life could flow with ease when I trusted my intuition. I realised I had been living without boundaries.

I prepared a list of boundaries. I struggled through this task as the idea of boundaries was foreign to me in terms of defining them. I was aware there were times when I knew I felt anxious and confused inside when someone had done something I wasn't happy about. I could now link these feelings of anxiousness and confusion to the act of someone crossing my boundaries.

There was a transition from past to present as I felt I was a new self, yet I didn't have any evidence of what my new life looked like. I had a blank landscape. It felt like I had my wobbly boots on. The vastness of being able to create what I wanted felt exciting and hesitant. I chose to embrace the wobbliness and the unknown. I needed willingness and a little bit of grit to travel my blank landscape and decide what seeds I wanted to plant.

The act of failing was removed from my reality. I realised events in the past I would have classed as failures were simply trying to teach me lessons and help me grow. It was easy to understand others and their behaviours and not take it personally when I looked for the lessons. I have received the greatest gift of releasing my limiting beliefs of rejection and abandonment through the way others treated me.

My relationships have cracked me open and I doubt the individuals involved will ever understand the depth of my gratitude. It is freeing to understand we are all on our journey and I am not responsible for fixing anyone else. It takes courage to own your bullshit and many others choose to never own their bullshit. I learned there is no right or wrong, good or bad and experiences are "it just is". We don't have any right to decide whether others' behaviour is right or wrong. All we can do is choose how we want to live and be treated and if others' behaviours don't fit our desires for our life, all we can do is let them go.

They, like us, are free to choose how they wish to live. There is pain in letting go of people you love but there is also beauty when you do it with grace, love and gratitude for the lessons you have learned. Naturally when we learn the lessons, the experiences helping us learn the lessons, leave our life with ease. I forgave myself for tolerating behaviours that hurt me. I forgave myself for staying quiet and not speaking my truth.

I now identified when others were bamboozling me in conversations. I likened it to wrestling with a pig. As quoted by George Bernard Shaw, "Never wrestle with pigs. You both get dirty and the pig likes it". I learned how to stay out of the mud and watch the pig get dirty in their filth. I was not trying to fix anyone. It was their shit, not mine. Once I'd found the courage to own my bullshit, I could stand on the edge of the mud pit and not get dragged in.

As I was feeling free, ideas were forming on how I wanted to help others break through from repeating patterns, and limiting beliefs and create the life they desire. I wanted to help others have confidence when making choices for their future and guide them to let go of fear and expectations.

When the twelve months were up, I resigned again from the job and accepted a part-time role working for a company I had previously worked for. The part-time role gave certainty to my human self in how the bills were to be paid and gave my soul the space to create my business. I wanted to be an activator of truth for others, igniting their connection to their soul and allowing them to choose themselves and live freely with ease.

I started my business Integrated Soul and began offering breakthrough sessions through my Facebook page. Jenny saw my Facebook post and sent me a message via my Facebook page. Jenny came to me because she didn't feel in control of her life and felt confused about what she wanted. We scheduled a discovery call to discuss what was going on for Jenny and how she was feeling. Jenny committed to my breakthrough session package to help her make changes and find joy in living again.

Jenny was grieving the loss of her dad and was wanting to leave her full-time job to start a business in her passion of human design. Jenny was feeling heavy, sad, insecure, confused and powerless. Jenny was lacking trust in herself and her power.

The breakthrough sessions were conducted over Zoom, and I helped Jenny identify her limiting beliefs and the initial root cause of when she developed each limiting belief. I then helped Jenny release her limiting beliefs and replace these limiting beliefs with beliefs she wanted to live her life by.

In her grief, Jenny has closed down her heart. I helped her soften and accept it was ok to feel sadness in times of grief and that it was also ok to feel happy in times of grief. I helped Jenny allow her emotions to flow and release them instead of burying them inside.

Jenny was carrying generational trauma and believed that to be true to herself, she had to do life all on her own. She believed it was not possible to be true to herself and also allow love and partnership. She was fearful of meeting a romantic partner. I helped Jenny define what she wanted in a partner and trust in herself to choose the right romantic partner when she was ready.

Jenny believed because she was single, she had to start her business whilst she was in a full-time job and was unable to quit her job. Her reality was she would never start her business if she stayed working full time as the full-time job consumed her time and energy. Jenny released this limiting belief, embraced her gifts and she became clear on how she wanted to live her life. She left her full-time job and started her own human design business. Jenny is now helping others understand what gifts they have and how to use them to become who they came here to be.

If you are ready to take action, I invite you to follow my Facebook page @Integrated Soul for more tips to help you be free.

My vision is to help as many people as I can to have their breakthroughs from repeating patterns, confusion, and agonising over decisions in their minds. I support clients to choose themselves and create the space to allow them to observe what is going on in their lives. I guide them to reconnect to their soul, own their bullshit, define their boundaries, transition through their blank landscape, and create the life they desire.

Are you ready to take ownership of your experiences, feel confident, see the choices available to you and create the life you desire? Do you want to do all this with ease?

It is time to choose you and leap. I know you are ready, and I am here to guide you on this journey by working together to transform how you live your life. I work with clients one-on-one or you can also join my waitlist for my upcoming break-free group program. To break free of your limiting beliefs and become clear on how you want to live and feel, book a discovery call or find out more about the group program by sending me a message on my Facebook Page.

It is time for you to find the courage to own your bullshit, be confident and live life being guided by your soul. Life is magical when you make this choice.

About the Author

Melissa Haggarty is the owner of Integrated Soul and specialises in coaching, animal communication, and energy and soul medicine. Melissa lives in Gladstone, Queensland, Australia, and also offers expertise in leadership and personal organisation drawing from her 20 years of experience in managerial and leadership roles in the industry. Melissa is a qualified Industrial Chemist, Certified Master Coach, Animal Energy Communicator, and Energy and Soul Medicine practitioner. Melissa loves helping business owners, leaders, and individuals ready to choose themselves, activate their truth, break free from their limiting beliefs, and create the future they desire.

Melissa loves camping in isolated spaces, either bush or beach. Melissa loves attending concerts and live productions. Her favourite activity is sitting on the deck watching the sunset. Above all, Melissa loves watching the magic of life unfold when she hands it over to the universe.

Facebook: @ Integrated Soul
Email: melissa.haggarty@outlook.com

Elizabeth Hood

Change a Little; Change a Lot

It was New Year's Eve December 2013 I found myself sitting in complete silence. Unheard of for what others would be doing on a typical celebratory night. I was determined to change my life, and at this point, I didn't care at what cost.

I'll be honest, I was miserable, and the future looked completely bleak to me. I grew up in a large family. 1 of 8 children and if taught anything, it was not to complain, and certainly not to quit. I married young at 20, and soon after found myself in a verbally abusive marriage. I had an innocent, high expectation of new love, which left me reeling – this was not meant to happen. I grieved for years. I spent most of my nights weeping to sleep, all whilst trying my best to learn my own identity, pretend it wasn't happening, and smiling fresh every day. This period continued for years, and I stayed silent under the belief that quitting was not an option. I pushed myself to stay strong, not only for myself, but for the sake of my 3 beautiful girls. I took them (and myself) out of the home as much as possible to avoid the anger and provide them with the peace I knew they deserved as children.

There were only 2 choices. I could continue to feel sorry for myself and choose a future of misery or choose to change myself and what I could personally control. The latter brought me to that night on New Year's, home alone and undoubtedly knowing I was not willing to enter another year without being intentional of the change I wanted to achieve. I was at a crossroads of my life where I knew the pain of staying the same outweighed the pain of change, and I was willing to do whatever it cost. Little did I know that you don't have to change much, to change A LOT.

That night I decided to dedicate 1 year of my life to study what it meant to be successful. I was hungry to take my life to the next level and I knew that there must be a common thread between those that lived a life that I determined was my definition for success. As I sat and wrote my goals for that year, I understood I would need to invest in myself sacrificing both the time I needed to learn and also finances for the resources from those that I wanted to learn from. I quickly realised that success leaves clues and that it is in the simplest layer of our daily routine that determines and directly co-relates to our output and achievements. Aristotle said "We are what we repeatedly do. Excellence is not an act, but a habit". It was through studying the lives of others, that I realized that the secret to our success lies in our simple, daily habits.

To change my life, I knew I needed to change my habits. I quickly identified 5 common denominators in successful people and decided I would spend that year practising these same daily habits and observing any change they had in my life – after all, at this point, what did I have to lose?

1. "5AM Club" – Get ahead of the game and start your day proactively by doing the following:

2. Gratitude – I listed the things I am grateful for every morning and my "I AM" Statements

3. Reading – I read a book a month and listened to a daily podcast – all self-developmental.

4. Exercising – ½ Hour every morning

5. Get a Coach (Choose one that best identifies with your area of required growth)

Looking at the above list, I knew I had no reason to make an excuse. Investing in a coach was well beyond our limited budget at the time, but I knew I had the means for tasks 1-4 and so decided to begin there.

Happiness begins the moment you keep the promises you make to yourself. It was the 1st January 2014 I began "changing the little things". By dedicating the first hour of my day to myself, I changed my life. During this period, I learned 84% of the subconscious brain filters thoughts through a negative lens. Unless we are proactively feeding our mind with the right tools for life, our brain reverts to the default position of negative.

Everyone invests time and money to feed and train our physical bodies, yet we often lack the stamina to put equal training into the most powerful tool we have – our minds.

That year, the only thing I changed was the "hour of power". I committed to myself every, single, morning. That year the results I achieved in Real Estate as a Business Development Manager (BDM) **tripled**. In 2015, I was honoured to receive 3 National Business Development Manager of the Year awards and thrilled to have achieved this in Rockhampton, a regional city. The only thing I changed that year was the first hour of my day.

We all know results in life are a direct reflection of the hard work, determination, and intentional goals that we each set. Fairy tales don't exist so there was no instant magic wand. It would be 7 more years before the first light at the end of that tunnel appeared.

Property Management has always been a passion of mine. Call me crazy, but I swear it runs through my veins like an addiction. Being a successful BDM and onboarding an average of 30 properties a month also had its disadvantages. Meaning, the more we grew, the more work I was in-turn loading on my colleagues. As a BDM, I brought in new properties for management but had no control how that new business was then maintained. It was then devastating to see the long hours I had spent winning new business unravelled due to lack of service. The investment of time to bring in new business is futile when you are losing just as many out the rear door. The true value of clients is retention, and my passion was about building long-term clients based on trust.

It was 2am one night, sitting (as an employee) at the office I had been a part of for 14 years and I looked around the room. No one, not another employee, and not even the boss was there. That exact moment I realized if I was willing to work this hard, with this level of commitment for someone else, then why couldn't I show that to myself? I knew there had to be a better option. Hard work never scared me. That night, I quietly packed up my personal items and no one ever noticed. I didn't resign until 6 months later, but that night, the clock in my head started ticking...

Elite Real Estate Rockhampton

At 34 years old, with 3 daughters under the age of 11, and a marriage that was in effect, non-existent. Opening a brand-new business was not something I took light heartedly. With a new (large) mortgage for a family home we had just built, and my husband self-employed, it was a massive risk. A few close friends suggested the idea, but to me it seemed an inconceivable thought.

At lunch one day, with a local business acquaintance, I found myself discussing the idea of change with her. I was sharing my frustrations committing to a business I loved, but no longer saw value in, nor did it offer further personal growth. She said, "What if?" ... 'What if opening your own business is actually easier than you think?" It was a question that left me with the gift of curiosity, and I decided it was time to really start looking into those answers.

Finally, I was "on that train". Sometimes the best place to start, is just begin. Like a fledgling wanting to fly, I was sure as hell going to learn to fly on the way down. I knew I had to come to the point of no return, and so on 25th November 2015, with no business plan in place, and not even a business name decided, I resigned from the job I had loved for 14 years and decided to embark on the unknown. Call me crazy, but I knew beyond a shadow of a doubt, it was time to back myself!

It was a whirlwind summer as I spent 6 weeks creating and designing my brand and the values behind the business. I had to create systems and policies from scratch, marketing and website content, and write landlord brochures. I slowly worked my way through a long checklist and started seeing the pieces fall into place, until... I suddenly reached a roadblock.

Finance. No one had prepared me for the difficulty when trying to apply for support when starting a small business. I had an unwavering belief in myself that this business could not possibly fail, but it was a harder task convincing others to believe the same. I would have had more luck asking the bank to fund me for a new boat, than asking for a mere $40k to fund me a small wage. The more banks I went to, the more depressing it became. I had prepared a business plan but even with my history in the Real Estate Industry, and the awards, no one wanted to look at me. I reached my 7th bank, a smaller local one, and hoped with the community values they had, they would give me a chance. No luck, however, the business owner offered to assist with my business plan and requested my permission to give feedback on what I had provided. Desperate, and thinking I had an 'in', I said YES. He came back to me several days later with the feedback that based on my business plan, I was scheduled to go bankrupt by the seventh month! I kindly told him that on month 7 when I was flourishing, I expected a bottle of champagne. It was another 'no'. I was not willing to give up.

I started exploring the idea of business partners and had several interviews with business owners that were willing to fund me. I was getting excited, this was happening... until I found out that they all expected 51% return with no active contribution to my business. For a mere $40,000, and with no active role in my business, they expected to have an even larger ownership than me. It was my turn to say NO (thank you). I knew how hard I was willing to work, and the hours that I would contribute to ensuring this business was a success, and I also knew the experience I had within the local industry was something that would be valued with what I was willing to give. I believed in my worth, and I wasn't prepared to give this away on a silver platter just because someone else had some money to spare. I was back to the drawing board...

It didn't seem right, I had a business ready to launch, and no funding to fulfil this dream. With just 2 weeks prior to the launch of Elite (I had already announced the business to the world), it was coming down to the wire. I decided to consider family. I was fortunate to have a brother who was also an entrepreneur and after several meetings with him and his business partner, we reached an agreement of a small buy in. My brother knew my work ethic and it was reassuring to know he did not consider the investment a risk. He knew me. He knew my will to succeed. He knew I wouldn't let him down – It was time to roll.

The first few months were always going to be the most challenging as I had decided to open the business with zero clients and build it from the ground up. My passion has always been to have long-term clients built on trust, and therefore buying a rent roll was never an option for me. With a non-compete in place, I knew I couldn't rely on any existing clients as a head start, so it was time to just make calls, and get in and do the work.

More roadblocks appeared (as they do). I grew the business organically as I worked from my laptop in my car. Unfortunately, my home location couldn't access the internet, therefore I found myself sitting in coffee shops, day and night with my laptop. I ended up drinking lots of coffee that year. McCafe became a lifeline when 10pm came around and other stores were locking their doors to the public. Maccas offered to lock me inside so that I could continue to work.

I knew the statistics of failure opening a small business, and for any number of reasons, it would have been easy to give up. At no stage, however, did anyone warn me you could actually fail from growing TOO fast, or having TOO much new business. By month 7, I already had 120 properties under management, and I was absolutely drowning (but I got my bottle of champagne-haha). My business plan outlined when I had 80 properties I would put on my first employee, but little did I know it wasn't that easy. By the time I employed someone, I was already running too fast, drowning in the workload, and lacked the time it took to stop and properly train someone.

Within the first 12 months of the launch of Elite, we celebrated 200 properties under management. People call it luck, but I must disagree. Opportunity is often dressed in overalls and looks like work. This is exactly how I defined that first year.

With a continual stream of new inquiries and new business, there was no way I wanted to let anyone down. Unfortunately, I sacrificed my own time, and that of my family's to ensure this business got off the ground. I didn't know anyone else that worked the insane hours I had, and it was a day-by-day decision to do 'whatever it took' to ensure this business didn't fail.

On the anniversary of leaving my previous job, unfortunately the marriage dissolved. Not even a year into a new business and now this had to be juggled. As someone who doesn't consider failure an option, it took me a long time to come to terms with making this decision. I knew however, I had tried everything in my willpower for 15 years to make it work, and I needed to learn to redefine what 'failure' looked like to me. I knew I couldn't allow my personal life to affect the energy and trajectory of the business. For the next 4 years, I had to learn the art of working long hours, balancing a (very) messy divorce, kid's custody, and at 38 years of age choosing peace over money releasing everything I had earned to date starting completely fresh again. I was left with a $65K legal debt and nothing to show for it other than my business which was still relatively new. One thing I knew I did have was the opportunity to start again, learn from mistakes, and work like hell building a future that aligned with my values. You cannot put a value on peace of mind.

It's usually the toughest times in our lives that push us to grow to the next level. I believe we need to identify in these moments of frustration or pain life is giving us a gift to maximise the lesson. I doubt we would change our lives, if we weren't pushed beyond our comfort zone. Breakthroughs are birthed in painful experiences, and it was one of these years that brought so much progress to the business.

After 5 years in business, I bought my business partner out of their share – YES! This baby was finally mine! I was overwhelmed with the support from both my clients and team. The decision was made to add sales to the business and time to transition the business of Elite being about "Elizabeth", to Elite being about the team. Management skills were not my strength, but it was time to make an internal shift so that I could drive the business forward. Until that time, I had struggled with 'handing' over the business because I had a false belief that if "you want a job well done, just do it yourself", Trusting someone to do it equally well, if not better than me was a serious challenge. Once again, I started reading...

Most would say it was unfortunate, but I would say it was fortunate I had a bad fall and fractured the base of my spine. I spent months in bed that year recovering from both that accident and a major shoulder operation. After months of studying management, I found myself in a position to do nothing, but trust my team. The remainder of that year taught me if you back the ability of others, they back themselves. I was amazed watching them rise when previously I would have doubted. It was a breakthrough point in the business, and for me in understanding the power of a team.

The story continues in 2023, the team is strong, and I am now free to pursue the growth of 'Elite' to new towns. Each New Year's Eve, I set goals and make small changes both personally and professionally with the intent that will have an impact both in my community and to the strong women in my world. It is not about the things we do rarely with intensity, but rather it's in the small, consistent changes we make in our lives daily that provide the secret to progress. Change something little and change it today. After all, you don't have to change much, to change A LOT.

About the Author

Elizabeth Hood is the Director and Principal of Elite Real Estate. Elizabeth was born in Port Moresby, PNG, and has resided in Rockhampton for 36 years. Elizabeth is Recognised nationally for her excellence in building a property management business, and with three accredited Business Development Manager of the Year Awards in 2014/2015. Elizabeth is a fast-rising star in the world of Property Management. With over two decades of experience under her belt, Elizabeth began Elite Real Estate to meet the need for an agency with a personal touch, built on relationships.

She is a single mother of 3 teenage daughters (and a cute cavoodle), and in 2021 Elizabeth welcomed a fourth (fostered) daughter into their family. As a strong women and leader, Elizabeth is passionate about supporting other women in her position and teaching women that 'their worth is not a negotiation'.

Website: www.elitere.com.au
Facebook: www.facebook.com/eliterockhampton
YouTube: www.youtube.com/@EliteRE

Sally E Lean, M.Ed

Moments of pride are not always while you are standing on the podium or riding a lap of honour around the arena after being awarded Supreme Champion Rider at a show. I clearly remember a snapshot of one chilly morning soon after I turned 17. Having changed to her day rugs, I let my beloved horse out of her stable and watched as she meandered off down the paddock. Feeling super proud and even more independent, I had just driven myself to the stable, having been granted my provisional driving licence the day before. My mother was never so happy to loan me her car to do the morning muck-out run myself while she could finally enjoy a relative sleep-in before work!

Having been given a pony at age six, which although it may sound rather spoiled, my parents were practical, working middle class people and I was not the coddled child that had everything done for me. Having my own pony, and later a beautiful Australian stock horse that I trained in dressage and show riding, taught me responsibility and focus from a young age. My passion for horses and riding, plus knowing that there was a beautiful creature depending on me to take care of it, kept me grounded and focused during my tweens and teens, which would otherwise have been far more tumultuous given the other events that swirled around me during those years.

Learning and growing together with my pony after joining Pony Club, we didn't just join an organisation to develop our skills, Pony Club was a community and offered a place/space to belong with other horsey kids, united by our love of horses and often by the fun adventures we'd have. It didn't matter that I was one of the quieter, more academic kids at school who was never going to be 'cool', on my horse I knew what we were capable of as a team and I was blessed to have been given a pony with a big heart and lots of character. Sadly at 16 I faced the complete heartbreak of having to sell my pony after 10 years growing up together to be able to afford an upgrade. Fortunate to have met a lovely mentor who took me under her wing, my abilities had outgrown my little bush pony and a heartbreaking choice (and life lesson) had to be made. With my new horse, I was no longer attending pony club for skills development, but more to get attendance points so I could represent our club at zone level and our zone at state and tri-state level.

My love of animals also led to a part-time weekend job cleaning kennels and helping with general duties at a local veterinarian clinic not far from home when I was in Grade 10. I also became known to some friends' families as a reliable babysitter. And when I finished Grade 12 I took on a part-time job as a 'checkout chick' at a local supermarket. Finishing G12 I was young, not yet 18 and when I didn't get the grade I wanted due to the impact of my parents fighting which was tough for our whole family that year, so I made the brave decision to go back and repeat G12. Feeling very small on the first day of school with all the whispering, another friend who made the same decision and I were left feeling rather unsure of ourselves, but as that year unfolded, it became clear that it was one of the best decisions I ever made. Firstly, because I was selected to ride dressage for my pony club zone, in a tri-state competition. It meant months of preparation, riding daily, no matter what the weather and lessons with an Olympic dressage rider to raise my, and my horse's abilities. I kept my job at the supermarket as I needed the money to pay for the lessons and high-performance feed for my horse.

Looking back, I am in awe that my parents let this crazy scheme go ahead, but I think they knew my level of passion and maybe felt guilty for the interruptions the year before, plus I promised to use my riding and job to keep me super focused on schoolwork – and I did. My horse and I finished mid-field at that dressage competition, but with all that it took for us to get there that year, it remains as a huge achievement and a memory I'm very proud of.

The second good news for the year was that I did graduate with higher marks in my studies and was accepted into the exact course and university that I wanted. I did it! It was time to be able to go back to another passion that had developed in middle school, languages. Sadly, financial reality meant that I sold my horse, packed up my trophies and sashes and put them on a shelf in my parents garage along with my teenage dream of going to the Olympics as a dressage rider, and I went off to university to pursue a Bachelor of Chinese Studies, with the original intention of getting into foreign affairs and maybe having the chance to travel and work overseas.

However, what seemed like an absolute winning year on the surface was also a year when a lot of unravelling took place. The self-motivated, fiercely independent, smart, capable kid started to feel like a ball of string after a kitten has been playing with it – dishevelled and unravelled all over the floor… The trigger was turning 18, which in Australia is the drinking age, I was going out drinking and clubbing with friends. Suddenly having teenage males, fueled by alcohol and hormones, so close and in my face. The in-control girl suddenly didn't feel so sure of herself, and her inner world started to fray. Unbeknownst to my parents, or anyone around me, I had kept a dark secret for many years… Not long after being gifted that pony, I was sexually abused by a much older cousin, who had spent a summer with my family, working at the mill my father managed. It would be decades before I understood and recognised the grooming that took place and led to the abuse. But at the time, my 6-year-old self had somehow decided it was my own fault, and even though I didn't really understand what happened, I just had a sense of deep shame because it was somehow 'bad', I then concluded that I was broken and dirty and no one would really love me if they knew.

So, I buried it deep and held that dirty secret for more than a decade. Instead, because I could no longer trust anyone, I became smart and strong and independent, creating a façade that hid the unsure, broken little girl behind a mask of perfectionism and striving to excel in order to feel loved and acknowledged. How lucky those two sides of my young self were to have the blessing of a horse in my life, a focus and a passion that helped bind those broken pieces together throughout most of her tween and teen years. Nearly three decades after the abuse, I discovered the Japanese art and concept of kintsugi – mending broken porcelain bowls with gold resin. For me, horses had been the gold that held the broken pieces together! And it would take more years working in and on my personal journey before I could fully grasp the deeper concept of kintsugi: the repaired bowl is considered better and more beautiful because of its flaws.

Did that teenager really unravel like a ball of string all over the floor? No. Did she feel lost and feel like it took a long time to find herself? Hell yes. Unsurprisingly given the research that I later learned; I ended up in an abusive marriage in my late twenties. Fortunately, it was short term as I had the courage to stand up for myself and walk away, despite the traumatic events that unfolded in trying to leave and having my life threatened. Again, I was blessed to have much-needed support from my family at that time. And I was already in the process of building a career for myself in school education, so it was a blessing to have to focus on my students and my work.

After my short-lived 'marriage', I decided to investigate something that I once heard about from chatting with an Australian woman in the immigration queue in Shanghai airport: international schools. Having spent an amazing year as part of my university degree living and studying in China, of course I wanted to go back. Little could I have imagined the incredible international adventure that was about to begin. For the following 10 years I would work in several international schools across China: Guangzhou, Beijing, Hong Kong, and back to Beijing. It seemed mind-blowing for a Caucasian Australian to be running Chinese programs in China, but my main role was to train my colleagues in understanding the western pedagogy behind the curriculum – the 'why' of our work. Traditionally Chinese teachers are trained to follow a textbook page by page so instead of a curriculum, all that was required was to know what page one had to be teaching by what date. Clearly with International Baccalaureate programs, and other western curriculums with inquiry-based learning, student-centred teaching and learning and interactive learning practices at heart, there was a 'great divide' that needed bridging!

During my second year of teaching in China, I was invited to help establish ongoing professional development for Chinese language teachers in ACAMIS (the Association of China and Mongolia International Schools) schools. Principals of these international schools were desperate to bridge the gap... So as the only foreigner on the team, I collaborated with the other two program directors, and we designed an annual professional development conference to be held in the summer break. Notably, this conference is still running more than twenty years later. Clearly, with a 'white' face and job title being Head of Chinese, it was startling to many the first time they met me, and it also meant that every participant in those annual conferences got to know me.

Some highlights of the first ten years working in China also included starring in a Chinese television series called "Foreigners in China". A television crew followed me around for two days and they produced a half hour program introducing my life and work in Beijing. It was fun being recognised around town and asked, "Are you that Chinese language teacher?", and, "Do you still drive that Jeep?"! In 2008 the Olympics came to Beijing and in one of those 'friend of a friend' type encounters, I met a producer who had moved to Beijing to set up for the Olympics and she offered me a job as an interpreter! Assigned to a crew of (local) driver, producer, cameraman and on-air personality, not only did I translate and interpret for stories and interviews, but I also helped set up a lot of the stories that went to air. It was an incredible experience to be right there on Opening Night, just outside the Birds Nest stadium with two of Australia's top tv personalities on a live cross stand watching the performers and athletes file into the stadium! And how surreal to have fulfilled my teenage dream of going to the Olympics, just in a way that I never could have imagined back then!

However, none of these amazing things would have happened if I had not been on my personal journey to overcome the abuse from my childhood.

I started participating in personal breakthrough programs, first in Australia and then in China – being the only foreigner in courses was totally daunting at first. I knew the whole room was curious about the foreigner sitting among them, but for the first few sessions I sat quietly. When I did eventually stand up and introduce myself (in Chinese), I blurted that I have a 'story' that my Chinese isn't good enough! Of course, everyone laughed, not *at* me, but *with* me. And thus began three incredible years of participating and volunteering in these courses in Beijing, usually being requested to directly support the American course leaders who would fly in to lead the big programs. The breakthrough in realizing that although my Chinese wasn't perfect, I was perfectly capable of making myself understood, helped me to realize I had two 'voices' and I could use both to make a difference. Another incredible breakthrough came when I realised that I had been operating in a context of being '*just* a teacher' and the kids in my class were '*just* students', so I created a context of being a leader who was teaching future leaders and as you can imagine that had a profound effect on how I went about my work, both in teaching students and training teachers.

The other incredible breakthrough and life 'tool' that I gained was to learn how to un-collapse any event (the 'what happened') with what I made it mean about myself (the added 'story' or 'meaning'). The event itself was in the past, but what continued to impact me in the present and in thinking about the future was what I had made it mean about myself!! O-m-g! This goes for all events – big and small – but obviously the biggest, darkest cloud from my past was the abuse as a 6-year-old. In being able to decouple the actual tragic event (or series of events in this case) from what I made it mean about myself was the key to self-empowerment! Three decades after the event the truth hit home: I had been living from a 6-year-old's mistaken context that I was broken and dirty and that no one would really love me – and that had coloured my WHOLE life to that point.

New possibilities and new opportunities kept arising as I burst more and more limiting beliefs… After returning to Australia for a year, I was head-hunted back to Beijing to develop and implement a teacher training project for the Chaoyang District

Education Committee (like the board of education). With a unique team-teaching model, the program trained 200 teachers and impacted the learning lives of almost 10,000 students within three years. After that contract came to an end, I was offered a job teaching high school Chinese at one of the biggest international schools in the world in Singapore. Why move from an executive role and go back to teaching in the classroom? It was a new opportunity to become more highly trained and experienced in cutting-edge language and education practices at one of the best schools in the world. No-brainer. Two years later I was offered the role of whole school Director of World Languages and in the following four years grew the language team from nearly 50 to nearly 70, growing the World Language (daily program) and implementing a $25 million Chinese immersion program in the elementary school. Not bad for a small-town girl who grew up thinking she was never going to be good enough in general and her Chinese wasn't good enough!

Since then, the impact of the pandemic has reached around the world causing seismic shifts for so many of us. I had moved to Bangkok, Thailand to work in a startup school with an innovative approach to education. However, having lost my darling Mum back in 2018, gone through a major workplace bullying situation and ending up with PTSD, a major fright with my Dad's health made me stop and reevaluate what was important.

So I chose to give up my multi six-figure work & well established career in education and finally managed to get myself back home to a very closed and locked-down Australia. What does one do when repatriating to a small, regional city after a high-flying international career? Well, first book six months of personal coaching with a great coach while you take a six-month sabbatical to do a reset and figure out what comes next. Then slowly figure it out.

The work my own coach led me through inspired me to think about taking on coaching. So I dived in and did my NLP (Neuro Linguistic Programming) Practitioner Training and soon followed that with Masters level training. In that first year I worked with adults, offering success, transition and confidence coaching to professionals wanting to follow their heart out of spirit-destroying employment and into the freedom of setting up their own business. Gradually though, I realised that I still want to work with young people – after all, they are our future leaders.

Why wait until they are adults to provide in-depth leadership training?

Bringing all my own diverse experience and all the training I've had from top education leaders around the world and adapting it to leadership and confidence coaching programs for high-achieving teens as well as communication and connection coaching for their parents. School based programs are coming soon; designed to support schools in developing the leadership skills of their high achieving students. Our coaching programs are also well suited for international and migrant families who often have cultural and language challenges on top of all the usual 'family stuff'. Children are often expected to live as though life will begin 'one day, someday' when they are considered to be an adult, but their lives are *now*. Instead of worrying about some uncertain future that may await them, and being buffeted by social media, let's start giving them more of the skills they need to be in the driver's seat of their lives, taking responsibility and taking the lead in their own lives today.

My soul objective is to have our teens *Lean In to Succeed.*

About the Author

Sally is the Founding Director of Lean In to Succeed, providing leadership and confidence coaching for high achieving teenagers and family communication coaching for parents. Sally has enjoyed an award-winning career, working in some of the top international schools in Asia and presenting around the world over the past two decades. Having worked with thousands of students from over 50 countries, empowering students is the core of her work at all levels, from teaching to teacher training.

As the Director of World Languages in one of the largest international schools in the world, Sally worked with and has been trained by some of the top education experts in the world. Fluent in Chinese, with a unique understanding of the East-West perspectives, Sally founded a $25M Chinese Immersion Program for her school in Singapore. She loves animals and has been blessed to be a rescue 'paw-parent' in several countries.

Facebook: www.facebook.com/LeanInToSucceed
LinkedIn: www.linkedin.com/in/sallylean
Email: sally@leanintosucceed.com

Lisa Lonsdale

The Quiet Achiever

The idea that some individuals believe they cannot start their own business due to a lack of skills, knowledge, confidence, personality, or courage has made me reflect on my journey. I aim to create a legacy for the quiet and shy people who might feel intimidated in school or social settings but still aspire to make something of their lives.

As an introvert, it took me time to understand the importance of stepping outside my comfort zone to grow and develop. Although it may seem cliché, this became a reality only after I started and established my own business at 32. The fear of walking into a room alone and not knowing anyone used to cause me anxiety, but now I look back on those moments with a different perspective.

I grew up on a property that was very isolated on the edge of the Hunter Valley in NSW, located two and a half hours away from any town. I did primary school through distance education and then onto boarding school for six years of high school. My family lived on a large rural property surrounded by mountains, and dense timber forest, with a crystal clear river flowing through the middle of the property. There was no such thing as the internet, we only got electricity in the late 1980s, and frequent power outages only added to the quietness of the area. Our phone was known as a radio phone, which was also unreliable sometimes. Our closest neighbour was a 45-minute drive, and while my parents tried to take my sister and me to community events, it wasn't a regular thing. Like most people on the land, going to town for groceries and to do business requirements was usually every 3-4 weeks.

My childhood has created the person that I am today. We are seeing things booming in agriculture now however, back in the late '80s, with interest rates over 20% and the crippling drought of the 90's, my memories are of the understanding that there was no extra money as my family was paying off a neighbouring property. My father and his brother were in a partnership, so once again, I learned what it was like to have family involved with the business. From the early 90's, drought struck, and our school days were shortened to half days to feed livestock. That seemed to be a monotonous job, and as a child, you become numb to the death around you of livestock and wildlife. I saw how my parents just kept going, and the option of giving up was never in our vocabulary, and it wasn't even on the radar to be discussed. I look back and always remember this, and that has made me so determined, and to an extent, I have been known as cold and hard when it was just a survival mechanism that we all had, figuratively speaking.

In between the bad times, there were some incredible memories, we had brumbies on one end of the property, and my sister and I would pretend we were the *Man from Snowy River* and chase them up and down the hills with our friends from boarding school or packing food in our saddle bags and going exploring for new waterholes on our horses and swimming in the river or creeks throughout the property.

Before we could saddle our horses my sister and I would just bareback and as long as we were back by dinner, our parents never questioned us.

As we got older, we found we could go a lot faster and further with a 4wd so this was added to our exploration as well. It was drummed into us from a young age that no one was going to save us in an accident so we had to be careful, our property was so steep in regions that if the vehicle left the road it wouldn't be stopped until it either hit a tree or straight to the bottom of a gully or creek which was hundreds of meters down.

As a child, I was incredibly shy and reserved, extending into my teenage years at boarding school. My mother even thought I was deaf in my early years because she often told the story of me not speaking until I was four, which I highly doubt is true. I was simply a timid and quiet child, and this did not change during my high school years at boarding school when interacting outside of my friendship group. I, however, am grateful for boarding school and the opportunities and friendships I still maintain. One of my biggest business mentors was my best friend from school when we were paired in the first week of school, and with her constant support and regular guidance, I would not be in business today. She often lifts me and encourages me to keep pushing forward when things get tough, and I provide a grounding influence for her when she needs support from a friend and a business perspective.

The concept of "normal" is subjective, and what is normal for me may not be the same for someone else. Our family has always joked that we have never been "normal," and I have embraced this by forging my own path in life and realising that banking and negotiating "corporate politics" wasn't for me and hence why Lonsdale Agribusiness was started.

It was not until my 30s that I realised that other people's opinions are not important and that avoiding negativity is key to preserving my peace of mind. This has sometimes meant letting go of valuable relationships, but it has been necessary for my overall physical, emotional, and mental well-being.

I lacked self-confidence in my early years, and even today, I still struggle with self-esteem at times. However, I have managed to improve my sense of worth. I used to believe that I had to accomplish everything by my 20s or consider myself a failure, but I do not know where this idea came from. No one close to me ever expressed this expectation, it was just something I focused on. I have always been very self-critical and put too much pressure on myself and the tasks I set out to accomplish. While this can be positive, it can also be negative.

At 40 years old, and with more life to hopefully live, I have realised that it was foolish to place so many time limits and plans on things that were out of my control when I was younger. It was not until I had children and gained a more meaningful outlook on life that I was able to let go of these unrealistic expectations.

My philosophy when entering an unfamiliar environment - do your best and be yourself. No one else is like you, so do not try to imitate others. Instead, be genuine, and others will appreciate your authenticity. Some may not resonate with you, and that is okay, because not everyone will be your cup of tea. This is why friendships and business relationships form - when two people find common ground and a mutual appreciation.

Building relationships, whether in business or in friendship, is about surrounding yourself with like-minded individuals. Continuously strive to learn and grow. It is not about being the most intelligent or the best, but rather having a willingness to learn and broaden your knowledge.

Time is a valuable resource, so make a point to invest some of it into improving yourself every day, by reading, listening to podcasts, audiobooks, or other learning materials. Challenge yourself and continue to learn, even if you think you know everything about a subject. Dedicate 20 minutes a day to reading, listening to podcasts or audiobooks, or improving your life skills. These skills can then be applied to your business dealings and interactions with others, such as asking for payment, setting fees, and handling difficult situations. Preparation is key, so take the time to get everything organised before diving in.

One thing I've observed as a mentor to others starting in business is the level of preparedness. It's great to have everything set up and in order before launching. It is a worthwhile investment of time and effort.

However, on the other hand, overthinking and overpreparing can prevent you from starting. Have confidence in your plans and get your contacts, networking, and communication efforts in place. Do not be afraid of making mistakes, as they provide valuable opportunities for learning and growth. Keep in mind that most mistakes can be fixed. Children have not developed fear yet and they fearlessly go after what they want. As adults, fear can often hold us back. So, have a go and don't let fear stop you from pursuing your goals.

Success in business requires a balance of planning and flexibility. While it's important to have a plan, sometimes things don't go as expected, and that can be a great opportunity to learn and grow. I find joy in solving problems for my clients and seeing their relief and satisfaction when a solution is reached. I may not have all the answers, but I am always willing to share my knowledge and assist in finding the information they need.

I get a rush from assisting others in their success. I readily acknowledge my limitations, but I am always eager to share my knowledge and teach others how to access information, even if I don't have the answers myself.

During the first four years of my business, I found it to be a difficult period in my personal life as well, which greatly affected my work. To cope, I turned to self-development and invested a lot of time and energy into it, using it as a form of distraction from what was happening in my personal life. This experience taught me the importance of balancing both your personal and professional life, as one can impact the other. Despite the challenges I faced, I tried to push through by immersing myself in work, though it may have made the personal situation more difficult. Nonetheless, it was what helped me get through a difficult time, specifically the breakdown of my marriage, which I prefer not to delve into in this context.

I believe that hitting rock bottom can be a valuable opportunity for growth and building resilience. Despite the challenges, it is crucial to keep moving forward and not give up. My experiences shape my character and make me stronger.

I am always striving for personal growth and self-improvement, and I see pushing myself to be my best as a fundamental part of my personality. In fact, my mother has noticed this tendency of mine since I was young. Although I am demanding of myself, I am not harsh towards others.

I have realised that success doesn't necessarily require being the best or the brightest at an early stage. Success is a subjective term, and people may measure it differently - some through wealth, while others through happiness and personal fulfilment. Speaking for myself, I am currently 40 years old and the happiest I have ever been. I have two wonderful children, and I am content with who I am. If only I could go back in time and tell my younger self in high school or my early twenties to stop worrying about the small things.

The biggest piece of advice I would give is to stop worrying about things that are beyond your control. This type of worry does nothing for your health, and if you suffer from anxiety, it only makes it worse. Instead of allowing stress and worry to consume you, you should channel that energy into positivity and find new ways to set and reach goals, take up a new hobby, or anything that brings joy and fulfilment. Although it's natural to worry, it's important to learn how to manage it. I have seen too many friends suffer from mental and health problems due to stress, and it's not worth it. If you find yourself consumed by stress, write it out, get rid of it, and move on with your life. Do not let stress control you - you are in control.

I have always had a passion for helping people since the start of my career. The feeling of accomplishment when a problem is solved, or a solution is found is what drives me. My friends might tell you that I'm not the best at remembering special dates like anniversaries or birthdays, and I'm notorious for planning parties at the last minute. But if you need help with something, whether it's personal or professional, I'm the person you should call. It brings me great joy to see the relief and happiness on someone's face after I've been able to help them. To me, this is my way of giving back through the knowledge I have acquired. If someone wants or needs help, I am more than happy to share my expertise.

I always repeat my motto, "you don't know what you don't know" whenever I give a speech or have a meeting with clients for the first time. It's important to remember that we can't solve problems if we haven't learned about them or haven't been in that situation. That's why I believe that you can't be an expert in everything and that spreading yourself too thin is not the solution. It's important to have a broad knowledge, but as in sports, the best teams work together by identifying each member's strengths and weaknesses, and if needed, they bring in someone to fill in the gaps. This is because in a team, you are only as strong as your weakest link.

From my experience starting a business, I learned to not overly focus on what my competitors are doing. Doing so can lead to losing your uniqueness and valuable time spent observing them instead of working on your own business. As the saying goes, *"be yourself as everyone else is already taken"*.

Remember to stay true to your principles and beliefs, even when money is tight. Making quick profits will only bring temporary gains. When I first started my business, I took courses from Bob Procter and Sandy Gallagher taught through Karen Brook, which taught me about goal setting and the power of positive thinking. By having faith in yourself and putting positivity out into the world, good things will come.

I recall a story from my school days when my mother and my best friend's mother enrolled us in a June Dally Watkins etiquette course. The most exciting part of the course was that we did not have to eat boarding school food as we learned proper table manners. I still remember the prawn cocktails being passed under the table to the girls who loved them, as it was a treat we never got at boarding school. Although some might say I learned a little from the course, I do remember the instructor's polished presentation and etiquette. It made an impression on me, even at the young age of 14. Presentation, no matter your budget, can make a difference in first impressions. It's essential to take the time to present yourself well, even if it takes a little extra effort.

I also believe in standing out from the crowd and being memorable, whether it's with a pop of colour, unique jewellery, and always a friendly smile. When you walk into a room, try to look relaxed, take a deep breath, and enjoy the experience. Don't be concerned about who is in the room or what they are thinking; everyone has their own issues to deal with, good or bad.

I will always be thankful to my parents for the wonderful upbringing they provided for my sister and me. It wasn't about material wealth, but about being raised in a warm, loving, and accepting environment. Despite my sometimes difficult, obstinate, and headstrong behaviour, they always showed me unconditional love and support. Their mentorship and the lessons they taught me during my upbringing have been invaluable and cannot be quantified. Their guidance has helped shape me into the person I am today, and I constantly strive to make them proud with my actions. I cannot express my gratitude enough to Graham and Deborah for their unwavering support and guidance throughout my life. Thank you.

To my children Mac and Harper whilst I don't elaborate on how important you are to me in this chapter mainly because I could write so much more than a chapter on how you have shaped me as a mother and a business owner. I hope one day you both will understand the decisions in my life I have made to make your lives better. And this is why I wrote a chapter for this book to show anyone who wants to know that life isn't easy, but it's worthwhile when you work hard and enjoy the experience along the way.

There are so many more life lessons and experiences that I could write about both personally and relating to business, as this is just a snippet to hopefully let that one person take the leap like I did and believe in themselves and start something new.

I wish you all the best and remember you cannot fail until you have tried and it's only a failure if you don't learn the lesson from your mistake.

Don't ever give up and remember there is no such word as can't and work out how to "do".

About the Author

Lisa Lonsdale was raised on a beef cattle enterprise 150 km East of Scone and South of Walcha in northern NSW. After studying Agribusiness at UNE Armidale, she headed north to pursue a career in Agribusiness finance across Southwest and Central Queensland. Eight years ago, Lisa established an Agribusiness consultancy business. Lonsdale Agribusiness has a focus on the needs of financial analysis, business planning and performance.

Over the past 20 years Lisa has held positions on AgForce committee boards and has been actively involved in Queensland Rural and Remote Women's conferences as a major contributor. Lisa is very passionate about agriculture and has freely given her time as a mentor for the Australian Rural Leadership Program and the treasurer for the Capricornia Catchments organisation. Lisa wants to reflect on her journey to start up her own business and what trials and tribulations she has learnt on the way.

Email: lisa@lonsdaleagribusiness.com.au
Website: www.lonsdaleagribusiness.com.au
Facebook: www.facebook.com/LonsdaleAgribusiness

Jordie Lynch

I, Jordana Kayla Lynch, must confess. This very chapter has been carefully dissected, overthought, flipped around, tossed upside down, turned inside out and scrutinised right down to the dots of each 'i' and the crosses of each 't' by my beloved brain. I promise you, it is the post-transformation version of me here sharing my story but old habits do indeed die hard. Wisps of a deep thinker and a self-confessed perfectionist still materialise in monumental moments and opportunities like this today but certainly not enough to hold me back.

Onward with my story…

Overthinking has been my default setting for as long as I can remember. It started to make a more significant impact on my life however when I graduated from high school in 2014. I donned a doe-eyed look behind rose-coloured glasses. I was ready for life, adventures, new experiences, a career. To the world I knew what I was doing, I mean, I was 17 and ready to take it on no problem. Deep down, I had no clue and it sparked such an overwhelming sense of fear that had me eyeing off the exit sign in every new room or situation I entered. Life quickly became littered with more questions than clarity, I was often feeling inundated with indecisiveness, and significantly slowed down by second guessing and low self-esteem. So many options, so much to experience, achieve and look forward to, but thinking and overthinking took the confidence right out of my first few steps into life post-school.

By 2016, life had binned my rose-coloured glasses and my doe eyes were now sleep-deprived as I progressed through a degree in psychology. This degree definitely egged my overthinking on as my awareness of the brain's inner workings grew stronger along with my need to analyse and overanalyse the simplest of things.

My overthinking has made me feel like I'm always lost in life's labyrinth, weathering my self-inflicted stress storms as best I can while trying to keep my sense of adventure and direction strong. It can be a bittersweet time. It has inspired countless moments of tail-chasing, umm-ing, ahh-ing, and agonising over such trivial things. I would keep getting stuck in the slow lane with a racing mind while the most inspiring blend of self-made go-getters whizzed by; a beautiful blur of confidence and charisma. I had come to understand that I housed quite the malleable mind, highly susceptible to being pressed into a particular shape and function by external factors. This pushed the importance of choosing my surroundings wisely to maintain a healthy headspace.

I was able to pour my overthinking into something productive when I was offered the chance to write weekly columns in my local paper across the space of six wonderful years. I embraced this chance to connect with my community, make someone smile, tug at heartstrings, empower, uplift, and hopefully make a positive difference in some way. I blended my big heart designed to want to help others with my big love for writing. It was often during this experience that my overthinking shifted into overdrive.

I would spend hours, sometimes days, every week around my paid job, study and downtime thinking up topics that were relevant and carefully crafting feel-good relatable pieces that could build a rapport with my community; that could make an impact.

My overthinking has felt like a power tripping referee over the years. Despite following all the rules and never daring to put a foot wrong, it would pull me up at every move and refuse to acknowledge my goals. It felt like the antagonist in far too many scenarios calling its accomplice, Imposter Syndrome, in from the wings whenever I started to see my own character's worth. The biggest struggle has been living with 'all-terrain' overthinking (definitely not a brag) where it's so effortlessly taken on thoughts of every nature, size and texture, and happily busied itself with blowing it all out of proportion. I felt like I was living life on a loop. Eat, work, overthink, stress, pre-sleep overthink, sleep, post-sleep overthink, repeat. It brought about severe doubts over whether I would ever be able to reach my dust-crusted dreams up on the shelf.

My brain was starting to abuse its power as my decision-maker. It decided that I shouldn't enjoy a spontaneous dance in the rain or I risk catching a cold. It decided it's best not to apply for my dream job because I don't meet all the selection criteria despite having what I need to be the successful candidate. It decided that people pleasing is always top priority or I wouldn't be liked and appreciated. Life with my overthinking was exhausting. The inner turmoil it caused had me donning a vogue-gone-rogue look, one that certainly wouldn't be setting any trends – ever. I'm talking messy buns of the birds nest variety and bloodshot baby blues brought about by sleepless nights. Then there were the slumped shoulders, tired of carrying the weight of the world and supporting a head harbouring a mind that just. would. not. shut. up. The what-ifs wore trails into the carpet from their regular visits during the night and made a habit of stirring my anxiety from its comfortable slumber. My frequent fretting about the mountains I had made out of molehills worked my heart into such a frenzy and tampered carelessly with my cortisol levels.

To someone else, taking a leap of faith was liberating, terrifying and thrilling all in one. To me, there always had to be a safety net. My brain would have to dissect every little detail like the distance from the ground, how far away the landing point would be, and weigh up every possible risk tied to this liberating leap. My overthinking was overshadowing moments designed to empower me and help me grow more confident in myself. It was making such a mess of things and I couldn't seem to find the energy or power to stop it.

With every obnoxiously loud tick tock of the social clock looming over my early 20s and as pressures piled up, I realised I was beginning to enter the territory of my greatest fears: wasted time and living with more regrets than memorable experiences. This was meant to be 'the decade' designed to settle into life, make the big decisions and the major moves, and take the greatest chances to pave a path I was destined for. The path I was stuck on felt more like a loop leading nowhere. It was unhealthy and unsustainable as my thoughts began to twist things around to take on an entirely different meaning. I felt so out of touch with reality and my sense of self but eventually, it was the most softly spoken thought in my mind that spoke to me the loudest. It told me I was spending too much time flitting between the past and future that I was absent from the present.

I was recycling old stories at social gatherings, worrying so much about things that hadn't even happened yet, my sense of fun was flatlining, and I had fallen out of love with the one thing that makes up a big part of my life purpose: writing.

Every blank page had become a playground that my overthinking thoroughly enjoyed its time on. When the blank page would finally gain some wordy decorations, the overthinking would edit it until it took on a totally different meaning and then it would be back to a blank page; purpose erased, story untold, and chance to make an impact - flattened. As I came face-to-face with what had to be my millionth blank page, it dawned on me that this was beginning to look like my life. My own life story was starting to feel like one big blank page. Yet there I was, with the pen, with the power, to create something beautiful, impactful and different for myself.

So I dug deeper to learn what had been holding me back. When I tuned in to my chatty mind for long enough, I started to understand that it actually came from a good place and held good intentions. It was like an overprotective guardian angel, whispering cautions and looking out for me in a big scary world when I was burnt out and vulnerable. Equipped with this new understanding, I was determined to change my relationship with my brain and hopefully begin to simplify my overcomplicated way of life and thinking.

Next on the agenda was to top up the self-worth tank. I wasn't born to be a benchwarmer, there was so much more to my story, to my purpose, to the future I want to move toward and the legacy I want to leave behind. I aspired to be out there with my newly renovated headspace exploring the world, making memories, ticking items off my bucket list, learning lessons (the good and the unpleasant) and celebrating every little win because they're much bigger in the grand scheme than what they first seem. I longed to be out there kicking goals with the other goal-kickers, taking exciting leaps of faith with the other leap-takers, and making positive change with the tenacious changemakers. When I shifted my mindset into an optimistic space, I found that the words began to fall together more naturally in my writing projects. I could also promote my purpose a lot easier both on the page and beyond in everyday life.

Taking action and overcoming hurdles has always sounded uber-empowering but my first small steps to making a change were terribly shaky, challenging, and didn't feel all that grand. Nevertheless, they were steps in the right direction and I told myself they were going to make the most impact. I knew I could grow from any seeds of doubt planted in my mind, I just had to nurture them a certain way to be able to bloom. This particular thought served me very well as I was learning, growing more resilient and getting comfortable with rejections or radio silences on my penmanship path. My mind had finally found peace in knowing that my worth wasn't determined by acceptances or rejections, it had to come from me, with kinder inner dialogue, and much stronger faith in my own abilities.

Instead of one specific event that inspired me to take action regarding my busybody brain, it was a series of smaller moments. They shone a light on a pretty dim reality if I kept letting my overthinking overpower me in all aspects of my life.

These pivotal points in time gave me the courage to look my two greatest challenges, overthinking and Imposter Syndrome, dead in the eyes and start doing the things they'd steered me away from for far too long.

I dearly cherished any miracles and wins along the way as they made all the setbacks worth it. One major miracle, in particular, came to me in the form of the beautiful and inspiring Donna Kirkland who you may remember from Voices of Impact Volume 1. At the time, I had just started my little content writing business, JK Writing, and she had remembered my weekly columns in the local newspaper. So during one of the biggest moments in her own career, Donna invited me into her mayoral campaign team as her content writer despite my being new on the professional writing scene. Her kindness, charisma, authenticity, vibrance, trust and palpable passion for making a difference in her community was so moving. More than anything, it was her belief in me to help share her story, her values, her vision and desire to make a positive impact in all that she does that lit a fire in me. I will be forever indebted to Donna for that experience as it helped to breathe new life into my seemingly dormant dreams and top up my sense of self-worth. I could feel excited and optimistic about the future again and reflect on this great honour whenever my inner dialogue turned negative. As my little side hustle started to adopt its own heartbeat, it gave me a whole new lease on life and confidence I hadn't felt for such a long time.

My friends and family have also been the most beautiful blessings over the years. They have supported me unconditionally, snapped me out of unhealthy thought patterns, and coaxed me out of my comfort zone when I've gotten a little too comfortable there. A recent scare taught me just how crucial it is to go for every opportunity that presents itself, take leaps of faith, be spontaneous, and always have an adventure to look forward to. Late last year, my mum found out she had Ductal Carcinoma In Situ (DCIS). Thankfully, it was a non-invasive form of breast cancer that a lumpectomy could remove but it knocked my family's world off its axis. It really hit home just how short and precious life is and that it must be lived to the absolute fullest. My mum is my world, my best mate, a fellow overthinker, and one of my greatest inspirations and supporters all bundled into one beautiful kind-hearted woman. Her strength, especially over the past few months, has really stuck with me and made me truly appreciate life beyond the confines of my brain. It has strengthened my desire to embrace the present moment with my loved ones away from my overthinking and learn when to let my heart speak louder than my head to make a genuine impact on others, in writing endeavours and in everyday life.

Despite my tumultuous journey with my mind, I know it truly wants the best for me. It is equipped with everything required to help me achieve great things, I just need to take much better care of it so we can work together better in the future. I've always felt like I've harboured an adventure-loving, nomadic mind that must be exercised daily or it gets cabin fever. This inspired my deepest kind of love for self-care, puzzles, podcasts and music, learning, hearing stories, writing, time at the gym or taking walks in nature, and distancing myself from the digitals. This was going to be my key to unlock a healthier mind; a healthier me.

I realise now that I had been the type to fob off burnout and ignore any calls to slow down from my mind and body. So whenever my mind would begin to get fidgety and feel the need to obsess and overthink, it was my sign for self-care. I will admit that I'm someone who always has to be busy, ticking items off my to-do list because that brings me great joy and a sense of accomplishment. But I can also acknowledge that it may work against me as an added pressure at times. A boundary must be set so it doesn't become something extra for my brain to obsess over. In order to soothe and simplify things, whenever my inner check engine light flashes up, I take the pitstop without question. I take a step back, allow the racing thoughts to slow and fall into a steady silence, and step into life again with a fresh rested mind.

I've been able to change the language I live by which also influences how I can make my impact. So, instead of worrying so much about being a people-pleaser, I can be community-focused and serve others through my time, donations, simple acts of kindness, and be there for a friend and my family. Instead of allowing little thoughts to transform into bigger thoughts that become too heavy to bear, I can choose to talk with someone, whether it's a friend, family member or a qualified health professional. Talking has been the biggest saving grace that has helped declutter my mind and lighten my load.

Across my three-steps-forward, two-steps-back, five-steps-forward type of journey as an overthinker, I've cherished a myriad of milestone moments and unforgettable opportunities that have helped me hold faith in my future away from overthinking. When I start to think myself into an 'I can't do this' or 'I'm not good enough' kind of mindset, I choose to remember the times I was so convinced I couldn't do something but achieved it anyway. I reflected on all those times my mind would fumble for any excuse to bow out of a brilliant experience or chance to make a difference but committed anyway. I bet those same experiences are the ones that have gifted me the confidence I needed to keep giving things a go despite fear and negative inner dialogue. With this in mind, I strongly believe that drawing upon certain lessons, energies and memories from the past can combine to serve the present and future beautifully.

Life is made up of experiences, encounters and challenges that make you who you are. They write your story. If you can share it with others and tell of the times you overcame the challenges, you can be a success story that helps to write another because impact is infectious. I have been so blessed to encounter many inspiring people, overcome my inner challenges that seemed unbeatable and experience the ups and downs of life's layout to get to where I am.

Everyone has it in them to use what has worked against them to work in their favour. I navigated many years of thinking I wasn't good enough, undervaluing my abilities, and never being brave enough to branch out beyond my comfort zone. I never imagined being able to get off that hamster wheel in my head but I did it, after years of believing it was normal to think in continuous circles so much. Ever since, I've been lucky enough to start ticking items off my bucket list, kick some major goals, repair my relationship with my mind and plan more projects for the pipeline to continue my mission to make a difference well into the future. If I can achieve this, I promise, you can too.

About the Author

Jordie Lynch is the founder of JK Writing and also enjoys her rewarding role in medical administration. With a Bachelor of Psychological Science and a Bachelor of Arts majoring in Creative Writing and Criminal Justice under her belt, she feels excited for a future in writing, crime fighting and helping others. Some of her proudest achievements include her weekly columns, publishing an article on Bravery in UK's Breathe Magazine, working with Donna Kirkland's team as a content writer, and receiving an award in 2021 from Queensland Country Press Association for best regular editorial column in CQ Today.

If she isn't cuddling her Beagle x Cavalier, Oscar, she's brunching with friends, spending time with her family, or getting lost in her crime shows, puzzles, podcasts, reading and writing. She calls sunny Central Queensland home and has big dreams to travel, make memories with loved ones and give back to her community.

Email: jordie.lynch280@gmail.com
Facebook: www.facebook.com/jordie.lynch
LinkedIn: www.linkedin.com/in/jordielynch

Cornelia Macvicar

It started when I got my first postcard. Intrigue was stirred up inside me of what it would be like to travel and do what the people on the front of the postcards were doing. So whenever my mum could make it to the top of the steep hill in the town centre of Airdrie, Scotland, where the Oxfam shop was, she would stop in and get me a packet of stamps.

The excitement of opening the cellophane wrapper, carefully separating them to make sure that they didn't rip and looking on the map at the back of my book to see where all the different countries were that the stamps had come from, before taking my glue stick and placing them in the correct pages.

On the map at the back of the book I had circled a country, I didn't know why, but something had drawn me to it. I didn't know anything about geography, I was only a child around the age of six or seven years old with a fascination for stamps, postcards and travel. The country was New Zealand.

Fast forward thirty years and a face-off with the Scottish Parliament, here I was campaigning to have my home compulsory purchased due to the re-opening of the Airdrie to Bathgate rail line.

To let you understand, when I got married to my husband Andy we looked around to find our perfect first home. We found a beautiful 3 bedroom house in a quiet cul-de-sac in a village just outside of Airdrie. The property was only one of ten in the street, the neighbours were amazing, the street was beautiful and we made our house the same. We had 2 amazing children, Alistair and Andrea and created a life way beyond our expectations.

There was an issue, all 10 properties were constructed next to the old rail line, which the local Member of Parliament was campaigning to get re-opened as part of their promise. This promise meant that we would lose our homes, our friends, our neighbours and our lives that we had spent years creating. Everyone was devastated, well everyone that had been told they were being compulsory purchased that is. In some ludicrous idea, they decided that it was beneficial only to take 6 homes and leave the other 4 and have a train every 20 minutes rushing past. Our garden fence was bolted onto the old platform and they wanted to take half of our garden and leave our house where it was, our garden wasn't that big in the first place. The value of our home would have been virtually non-existent, as nobody would want to buy it with the plans they had. I had no choice, I took action and set up my own campaign for them to take all the homes and not just 6 and I won. The details of it can still be found on google today.

The story doesn't end there though, as this then brought about another dilemma for our family.

Where do we go now?

My husband Andy had been on a night out with a friend David aka. Tartan Terror who was emigrating from Glasgow to Bribie Island, Queensland. On his way home there had been a sign for an emigration seminar, he put his details in and the next day he received a call to ask him some qualifying questions. Andy was a bit confused as he had totally forgotten that he had done it, but quickly got chatting to them and found out that we could get to South Australia if we gained another 15 points. They asked if he had any family in Australia, he said sadly no, I smiled and said that I did.

The whirlwind commenced. I contacted my dad's cousin Gordon whom had left Glasgow many years before. We had met on a number of occasions and was more than happy to sign our papers, but unfortunately, he couldn't, it had to be a first direct relative. Enter Melissa aka Mel, she is the most beautiful human I have ever met and I am not saying that because yes, she did sign our papers, but because she is the most beautiful human I have ever met. I had never met Mel before and we travelled to Australia for a few weeks to have a look around in 2007 to make sure it was what we all wanted, children included who were 5 and 9 and the time. Both Mel and I were nervous wrecks, we didn't know what to expect of each other. What if we didn't like each other? But we had nothing to worry about. Mel is the sister I never had, we chatted for hours, days, weeks and beyond. We had the best time. When it was time to go home, our kids cried and wanted to stay with Mel and for Andy and myself to pick them up again when our visa arrived, cute eh?

On the 2nd March 2008, we arrived in Australia to start our new journey. We got a rental property with the help of Gordon who went to see it for us while we were still in Scotland, which was a huge help. We started furniture shopping for the things that we didn't bring, which I so wish we had. (Note to anyone thinking of emigrating, bring everything, your taste doesn't change and you end up buying the same style of furniture as you already had).

On the conversation of furniture, we went to buy a new lounge and dining furniture in the sales before we left Scotland and wanted it put straight into the container. I don't know if you are aware, but the name that you see a piece of furniture called pre-sale is different when it is on sale, that way you can't go back and say that you bought it last week for "x" amount. Anyway, Andy and I advised the salesman of what lounge we wanted and that our shipping company would pick it up as we were moving to Australia. The salesman asked where in Australia, we replied Adelaide. The salesman laughed and shouted on another colleague and asked him to verify what the lounge was called before it was on sale, to which he replied, wait for it "The Adelaide".

I've got another for you, we were so busy with organising and telephone calls, trying to catch up with everyone as we had made a promise to Andy's dad Charlie that when we got our visa we wouldn't drag things out. So we made plans to leave within the month of getting our visas. You can imagine how hectic our lives were, can't you? We had a few days out that we went to and a few that we had to cancel, we had to prioritise things. One of the days that I cancelled was a clairvoyant, I am not that into them, I have never been to one and decided it wasn't that big a deal if I cancelled. It had been organised with a few of Andy's family and I made the call to the gentleman and said sorry, not this time. He was fine, I didn't give any details, just said I was too busy. Just as I went to hang up, he said good luck in Adelaide. I said, "Excuse me?' And he said it again.

I spoke with Andy's family and they hadn't even been to their appointment yet!

We had settled into Australian life, kids were making friends and loving getting to play outside. It was such a novelty for them. We had a rental property with a swimming pool and there was a trail of clothes from the front door to the garden as they stripped off on their way through. It was hilarious to watch and I smile now thinking back to it. They were in football clubs, netball clubs, cricket, surf lifesaving, skate boarding, horse riding and dance classes to name a few, they were having the time of their lives. Andy and I even got in on the action by getting our football/soccer licence and helping out at the schools and local clubs. I even started my own cleaning business and was getting contracts from big companies and government organisations, I had to take staff on to help me out it was incredible.

We had always planned to go back to Scotland for a visit in 2010, as there were a few big birthdays that year. What we didn't know was it was going to be a big year for us too.

10 June 2010.

This date is etched in my family and friends souls forever. I was organising all my workload, making sure that the staff knew what jobs they had on all sides of the business for residential, commercial and building. That way I knew that I could go away to Scotland and all clients were taken care of.

There was only one last thing to do, which was the last couple of jobs that I brought a friend in to take care of them whilst I was away. They were doing me a favour and I loved spending time with them on the lead up to my break. Mrs B is funny and bubbly, we always have a laugh together whenever we see each other and she was the perfect fit. We had finished our work and were heading home for the day, chatting and laughing as usual on the drive home, sitting at traffic lights on a quiet, sunny afternoon. What happened next still shakes me to the core and I have no idea how it happened.

Mrs B and I were looking at each other laughing, then there was a noise. We came to a halt at the opposite intersection facing in a completely different direction from where we initially were. We were screaming. It was the weirdest feeling. Life was going so fast, but so slowly too. I got pulled out the car and sat at the side of the road and all I can remember is a pair of man's boots, I couldn't lift my head, I was shaking so much. I don't know what happened to Mrs B, I don't know where she went.

Andy cared for me as much as he could, waking me to take me to the bathroom and listening to me screaming as he was moving me, knowing that this had to be done before giving me more pain relief and letting me sleep again to heal. What developed during that time and took everyone by surprise was that I started having seizures and losing my memory. Following numerous visits to specialists and doctors, they said I had no memory recall, it was lost.

We had people dropping flowers off that I never seen as I couldn't move, others dropped food off which was generously accepted and we are eternally indebted to you for this. Andy was trying to work, look after the kids, look after me, cook, clean and shop. He was thrown into turmoil, I can't imagine what that must have looked like for him. His life stopped, and he took over mine.

Our young children had to grow up fast. Alistair was 12 years old and suddenly had to be the man of the house, as Andy had to work away to make up for 2 incomes. Andrea was 9 years old and without the help of her friend Freya's mum Deb, she would not have been able to attend any of the past times she enjoyed. We tried to protect them as much as we could from what was happening in our lives, but there were just things that spilled over and drowned them as much as it did us. The accident didn't just happen to me, it happened to all of us, but I didn't see that at the time and for that I am eternally sorry.

Fast forward 12 years, I have been seizure free for around 6 years, touch wood. My memory is a little better with the help of the alphabet system. If I don't remember the name of something, I go through the alphabet till the first letter is triggered and hopefully the word comes through, failing that, I go through the alphabet again for the second letter. A lot of family memories are gone, from things that we did together or when the kids were little.

I did find this very distressing to start with, but I am at peace with it now, knowing that there isn't a lot I can do about it. Perhaps one day they will all come back.

Talking about fast forward, I do tend to get out of the way as quick as I can if I am in the vicinity of a truck. It took me 5 years to be able to drive again because I had to be seizure free and then once I was able to drive, I used to hold my breath whenever I was going past one. Hearing the noise of breaking glass, seeing car accidents on television freaks me out and also hearing the screeching of tyres, which is strange because there weren't any at the time. The brain is a strange thing.

I had my first proper day out to Ikea of all places with Andy and Andrea, I had never been before and didn't know that each section took you into another, with one way in and one way out. Not the best place to have a panic attack and every exit sign you see takes you into another section with no way out!! I can laugh about it now, as did Andy and Andrea did at the time, they didn't realise what was going on. They just seen me stomping ahead, fingers tapping together and making my way towards every exit sign that I could see, trying to set off the fire alarms as I was trying to get out of the emergency exits. Such is life, not a place that I really want to visit in a hurry again, online shopping is a revelation as far as I am concerned.

With many of the specialist appointments came disappointment and being told that I would never work again was one of them. To be told that if I did work again, it would be a job with no great significance. To come from running my own business, which had been increasing in volume, to not being able to work was heart breaking. Even though it is no longer trading, I still get calls about it today. I have had a few online businesses as I am a great believer in self-care, you could say I am addicted to it. I think everyone should take some time out of their week to do something for themselves that makes them happy and is good for them too.

I am a fighter and very stubborn, I like to prove people wrong about me and work was one of them. Since I was 12, I have worked and I was going to make sure that the rest of my adult life was going to be no different. In 2015, I studied to become a Real Estate Agent and succeeded. In 2017, I worked as an Admin Assistant within the No1 Building Insurance Company for South Australia. In 2020, I worked as a Tax office for the State Government and still doing it.

How's that for no great significance?

As I had a business before, I always have that bug to be my own boss, which is why I dabble in online sales. This is where I met the lovely Melanie Wood in 2020, she reached out to help me and be my 'authentic self'. At the time I thought I was ready and tried really hard, but I was fighting against myself. I was too worried about what everyone else thought and how I would appear on camera, what would I say?

Today is different, everyone is doing their own thing to be worried about what I am doing and to be honest even if they did laugh or say something about me, I'd probably forget about them in a minute anyway!

Live your best life, and make self-care your addiction. Only you really knows what you are capable of and the lengths that you are willing to make to reach your goals. Don't let anyone tell you that you can't do it and take time out for yourself and practice self-care. This is such an important step in developing confidence in yourself and loving yourself. Go on and do it for you, you deserve it.

About the Author

Originally from Scotland and now residing in Adelaide, Australia, Cornelia is loving life and living life to the fullest. With a love for the outdoors, she loves nothing better than spending her free time in her garden and asking her family if she is a 'farmer' as she has started growing her own fruit and vegetables. She loves nothing better than spending time with her two children, who are a huge part of her life. Cornelia is an animal lover, especially her beautiful dog Layla whom is her companion and can't move an inch without her by her side.

With empathy being a strong part of her character, she has been involved in various fundraising efforts for numerous charities. She is looking to embark on the creation of a charitable organisation collecting no longer used eyeglasses and make them available for low income and people experiencing homelessness. If you believe that you could help or are interested in finding out more, please reach out to Cornelia.

Facebook: www.facebook.com/cornelia.macvicar
Instagram: www.instagram.com/selfcare_addiction_cornelia

Christine McTaggart

Favour That Lasts a Lifetime

It was the winter of 1862 in Frankfurt Germany. My great-great grandparents with their eight young children, were keen to get away from the Prussian War and avoid the conscription of their sons to "cannon fodder." They made it through the snow to Hamburg to catch the boat to North America, but that ship had already set sail by the time they arrived. Sadly, that ship sank enroute to New York.

They decided to catch the next boat to Australia and on a promise of a farming job, they arrived four months later to a sparsely populated settlement in Rockhampton, Queensland. When the farmer saw the large family, he did not proceed with the promised job. Life was tough. Soon after arriving on the banks of the Fitzroy River in Rockhampton, they sadly buried their youngest twin son who had died from dysentery. After a few years, they acquired some land near the mountains and started an orange orchard and a pumpkin farm.

Gold discoveries at Mount Morgan in the 1880's brought many people to the region. My great grandfather Eustus moved to Mount Morgan, chasing the gold. The Salvation Army arrived in Mount Morgan too with their lively street meetings accompanied with tambourines, drums, and trumpets. Eustus and his family joined the Salvation Army. He recorded in the family bible, "saved from sin at age 36". The Salvation Army became a part of the Werner family.

I am a fifth-generation descendant of the Werner family. My grandfather and father were country saddlers. Werner's Saddlery in Rockhampton was known far and wide for their excellent Werner Wonder Poley saddles. Pop Werner survived through many lean years, but when the American soldiers set up their army bases in Rockhampton in 1940, he started to boost his income by making leather pouches and bags for the soldiers. In 1940, General MacArthur came into my grandfather's saddlery shop to buy a leather knife pouch. He said, "Robert, you are lucky you are not in Germany, or you would have been lost in the gas chambers of the holocaust."

At our childhood home, every child was expected to work. Most mornings, my younger sister Robyn and I would sit with our father on the front veranda whilst he repaired saddles. We would tease out burrs from huge piles of horsehair, so that our father could stuff it inside the saddle he was repairing. He worked long and hard. Both my grandfather and father made up to six saddles a week and shipped them all over Australia and beyond.

We did not have television at our house, as dad thought we should put all our time into our school studies. However, my wonderful Nan Werner lived just around the corner, and she had a big television and lots of treats. We would run to her house after we finished our piano practice. Nan was the kindest person I knew. She loved me so much. I can still feel her love all these years later.

When I was fifteen years, I had a choice to make. I could take a job in a local public service office, or I could go onto Year 11. No girl in my wider family had ever gone past Year 10. I made the choice to stay at school.

After Year 12, I received a Commonwealth scholarship to study at any university. However, no girl had ever been to university in our family. Thankfully, the regional college in our city had just opened a primary teaching course. I started my studies in the education field.

My father was good friends with the local politician, and he wisely encouraged me to start studying a Bachelor of Arts at the University of Queensland as well, through distance education.

This wise advice opened an amazing opportunity for me when I was a young teacher at Blackwater. I completed both my Arts and Educational Studies degrees whilst teaching in the bush.

Towards the end of my third year in Blackwater, I was flicking through the Gazette for job options. I saw an advertisement for a Guidance officer training program at the University of Queensland. I barely knew what a guidance officers' job would entail, but I applied anyway. To my astonishment, I was accepted and started the post-graduate course preparing for work as a high school guidance counsellor. The extra degrees that I had achieved were the key to opening this incredible opportunity.

I got married at 31 years to Andrew. A few months later, I was diagnosed with a very serious melanoma on my hand. I had sought advice from a few doctors over the year about the mole on my hand. Even on my wedding day, I put a lot of make-up on the mole to cover it. All the doctors had told me, 'That mole is nothing to worry about."

My younger sister, Dr Robyn and her family arrived home on their annual visit from Western Australia. She took one look at my hand and advised that I should get the mole off as soon as possible. Her advice saved my life. Due to the seriousness of the melanoma cancer, the specialist advised me to wait three years before starting a family.

Shortly after, my husband Andrew fell off a sailing boat in Keppel Bay. The wind blew the boat back to the shore, but Andrew was not on it. He was a non-swimmer. I ran to get help. I remember the hopeless feeling as I looked out over a wide expanse of blue ocean. I thought, "I have just gotten married and now he has gone." To my surprise, I saw him walk out of the ocean up the beach. I could hardly believe he was alive. The life jacket had saved his life.

At 34 years of age, our first son was born. During the pregnancy, I was referred to the Senior Obstetrician at the hospital as I was considered a geriatric mother. All went well and I went on to have a further 4 babies with the last one being born when I was 42 years. I have loved every minute of being a mother.

It has taken every ounce of energy, but I believe my life's best treasures are my children and now my five little grandsons. I have taught my children that we are the givers in life. We are not the takers. In every situation, where we were experiencing a big need, I have explained that we will give to someone else's need first and then we will look for a wonderful outcome for our need.

After our fourth child arrived, we urgently needed a bigger car to get around. With very little spare money and one income, finding a second-hand Tarago car was almost impossible in our regional town. One afternoon I was walking through the local shopping centre.

Up ahead, I saw a Salvation Army man collecting funds. I said to my little son, "Let's give some money to the Salvation Army." When I opened my purse, I could only see coins. I gave all the coins to my son to give to the Salvation Army man.

I asked my son, 'What need do we have?"

He said, "Mum, we need a Tarago." Even though these coins we were giving were such a small amount, we agreed that this gift was a seed for the big need we had.

On the next afternoon, my eldest son and I were driving home in our small sedan. We pulled up at the traffic lights. Immediately in front of our car, we saw a blue Tarago with a For Sale sign on its window. I said to my son, "Write down that phone number." Within a day we were the happy owners of a very good Tarago.

A close friend saw me driving the Tarago the next day and said, "Is that car for sale?"

I said, "No, I just bought it!" He said, "I have been chasing that car for weeks trying to buy it." I was so thankful that the seed we had given to the Salvation Army had resulted in such a miraculous provision for our need for a bigger car.

The concept of giving into a need is such a part of our family now. I have many stories that illustrate this principle, that 'the generous prosper.' If we have a need, we find someone first who has a greater need, and we give to them.

I have taught my children to work hard and look for opportunities to excel. When my eldest son was completing Year 12, he applied for medicine at James Cook University, Townsville. 2000 students applied for the 150 places available in the Bachelor of Medicine and Surgery course. It would take a miracle to gain a place.

We drove 750 kilometres north of Rockhampton for the university interview. Both of our cars were very old. We set off in our small green Mazda. We were just past Ayr when the car heated and stopped abruptly. Smoke was pouring out of the car. The engine had blown up. A tow truck took our Mazda away. Thankfully we were able to hire the last car in Ayr. We stayed overnight at a Townsville hotel. However, at five am the hotel fire alarms were blaring for immediate evacuation. My son grabbed his computer and suit. Nothing was going to prevent him from getting to the university interview.

The interview went well and on Christmas Eve, my son was offered a place in the six-year medical course. Student accommodation was very tight at the university. We visited the George Roberts Residential Hall, but the receptionist told us that there were no vacancies for the following year.

I walked away, wondering what I should do. I decided to send a donation to Teen Challenge. I knew they helped young people in need of accommodation. My son had an urgent need for university accommodation. In a few weeks, he received a letter offering accommodation at the residential College. Giving a gift opens miraculous doors. I will never stop giving, as it opens the way for the impossible to happen. The favour of God had opened a wonderful pathway for my son.

When one of our sons was in Year 10, I took him on a three-week trip to Egypt and Israel. This was a huge step. Our family had barely been further than the local beaches, as travelling with five young children was challenging. This trip opened the door to travel for us. In the years following, I would try to take each of the five children on adventures to different locations all over the world.

When my daughter was studying Oral Health Therapy at the local University, I realised I had only a few years left with her at home. Every June, we would travel to places that we had only ever dreamt about. We went to places like Jordan, Greece, Finland, Israel, and Estonia. One time, I took my daughter and youngest son on a nine-day rail trip in Switzerland.

From the small hotel in Lucerne, the tour guide walked us to the local railway station to begin our trip. We arrived at 7.30 am. The tour guide asked us to take out our train tickets. She had given us a ticket on the previous day, but I thought it was just for that day's train travel. Little did I know that the ticket was for the entire trip and was worth over a $1000. The train was due to leave at 8 am. I asked my son if he had his ticket. He said, "No." I asked my daughter if she had her ticket. She said, "Yes." My daughter always puts everything in her big handbag.

I did not know what to do. I quickly prayed to God for help. I saw a taxi close by. My daughter stayed on the train platform. My son and I jumped in the taxi and asked the driver to take us to the hotel. I did not know the name of the hotel, but I knew it was about four streets away. We arrived at the door of the hotel and ran into a packed foyer. I called to the receptionist for help. She said to go up the lift and check the room.

We squeezed into the very small lift to the second floor and then ran to the room. We saw the cleaners standing at the door of our room. Frantically, I searched in the bins and there I saw one train ticket. I searched under a bed and there I saw the other ticket.

We raced back to the taxi and drove to the station. I quickly paid the driver, and we ran along the platform hoping the train was still there. We got there just in time. Everyone in our group cheered as we reached our seats. A few minutes later, the train departed the station, and the very efficient ticket collector came by. He said, "Tickets please!" I was so thankful that we had found those train tickets.

In every challenge in life, I pray to God for wisdom. I have taught my children to always pray for wisdom too. I have endeavoured to read a chapter of Proverbs in the Bible each day. There are 31 chapters in Proverbs and the wisdom in these words has brought practical help to tough situations.

Making wise choices helps to create a calm, happy life. I have taught my children wise principles for life. I would write out proverbs on pieces of paper and stick them on the kitchen cupboard. We would memorise the proverbs at tea around the kitchen table.

One of our favourites was from Proverbs 16:24: "Kind words are like honey, sweet to the soul and health for the bones."

I recounted family stories from previous generations to inspire them to work hard, to be honest and to seek for the wise path. I started writing daily inspirations, so that the stories of the wider family would not be lost. I wanted to pass on the wisdom and heritage of faith in God to the future generations.

I published six inspirational books titled "Today Is". Each morning I would think of a name for that day. For example, Today is the day for hope; Today is the day for joy; Today is the day for laughter. I would write out the inspiration that I felt for that day. After I had 30 inspirations, I self-published them in small books. These books are available on Amazon.

One of my dad's stories was included in "Today is" Volume 2. Dad was returning from deep sea fishing at the Keppel islands. He left his boat on the beach and went to get the trailer, but the tide was quickly rising. Dad's boat trailer got bogged in the soft sand at the water's edge. It looked like a disastrous situation. Dad said a prayer to God for help. He looked up and to his utter surprise, he saw a tow truck coming along Fisherman's beach. He waved the driver down and soon his car and boat were safely on dry ground. My dad said that he had never seen a tow truck on that beach ever before. It truly was a miracle.

I have taught my children to never take offence in life and to be quick to forgive and let offences go. Sometimes, raising teenagers takes every ounce of wisdom. Random acts of kindness can help. We may not like their behaviour and we may just want to keep nagging them to change their behaviour. However, putting a chocolate bar on their pillowcase without saying too much assures the teenager that they are loved, no matter how bad the situation is. Your kind, wise words can shape their future.

I have taught my children to look for adventure in life, to take some risks, to go to lots of places and learn new skills. It is good to push yourself beyond what you think is possible to achieve and look for unexpected opportunities coming your way. I have taught my children lots of sayings, (for example, the best help is at the end of your own arm, or the shortest pencil is better than the longest memory).

My life's work has been to create pathways and opportunities for teenagers in schools.

I have always wanted to open doors for others and to never be a person closing doors. My career in school counselling has been more than a job. It has been my passion to listen to the students and the families and to assist them to move forward towards their dreams and aspirations.

So many students have come back after school and said to me, "You helped me so much, you saved my life, and you gave me good ideas to consider."

Now people ask me, "When are you going to retire?" I never want to retire from doing good and speaking positive words to those around me. People need hope, joy and kindness.

Some of my recent projects are in sponsoring widows in India and Bangladesh to start-up businesses to provide for their families.

Bringing help to the vulnerable is so important. We live in the lucky county here in Australia and we should do everything we can to alleviate the suffering of those near to us and those who are further away.

GIVING IS THE KEY TO SUCCESS IN LIFE.

May each of us seek to live a life in the service of others. I love this quote by John Wesley.

"Do all the good you can,
By all the means you can,
In all the ways you can,
In all the places you can,
At all the times you can,
To all the people you can
As long as ever you can."

Christine McTaggart

About the Author

Christine McTaggart is a mother to five young adult children - a doctor, an oral health therapist, a business entrepreneur, a mechanical engineer, and a secondary school teacher. In the past two years, she has been very happy to become a Nana to five little grandsons.

Christine is a high school counsellor with over 30 years' experience in Queensland schools. She has travelled to many interesting destinations around the world, including Iceland, Israel, Ireland, Istanbul, and the Cook Islands. Christine has written six inspirational books titled "Today Is" by Christine McTaggart (available on Amazon). She loves swimming and walking the beach. She has sponsored many children through World Vision and Compassion Australia over the years. Christine believes that life is all about being a giver. Good always comes to those with a generous spirit.

Email: acmct7@gmail.com
Facebook: www.facebook.com/christine.mctaggart.12
Phone: 0430187361

Leanne V McVeigh

The Corporate Therapist

A latecomer to the Mental Health Services Industry in Australia, I opened an online Therapy practice, for professionals, in Clinical Therapies in 2022, after completing 2 years of study through a London College.

My professional background, until then, had been in Banking and Finance and Criminal Law, in senior legal administrative roles. I have worked with C-Suite professionals all of my career. From working with a Managing Director of a Bank to a Senior Criminal Lawyer at the Criminal Justice Commission. The biggest team I managed was a team of 12. A combination of senior police officers and lawyers, with my own two support officers and all whilst supporting my husband in our sole partnership, in back office duties, bookkeeping and all written correspondence.

Business Professionals, Business Administration, business creating and the nurturing of others, was always in my life path, all were to come together and to play important roles in founding my new global online therapy business The Corporate Therapist, specialising in trauma and stress, among the professional sector.

Looking back, before it all began, back in 2020, with the beginnings of the Global Pandemic in full swing, with various countries and states in differing stages of lockdown and daily, fear based, bombardment on all social media platforms, which was very hard to ignore and process. Little did I realise how the pandemic made such a substantial impact upon my work and family lives. We were in lockdown and all living, working and schooling, in the one premise and just like the rest of the world, we waited with bated breath and a great deal of anticipation, for when it would all end, so we could get on with our lives. During this time, I was glad I had my family close by and I was also glad I was studying a rapid non drug clinically researched lasting treatment for mental health issues from phobias through to PTSD, that I could use for my loved ones and colleagues, during this unprecedented time. What were the chances?

The hours were sometimes gruelling, especially in winter when I attended live lessons at 1:00 am and 3:00 am AEST (Australian Eastern Standard Time) and then I would go to work for the rest of the day. I did sneak in a nana nap here and there some days. I remember once putting my head down, on my desk, for a little rest and waking up 20 minutes later.

My first practical buddy, was an older Psychiatrist, who advised me on how lucky, we both were, to find this course and we were also so so lucky to now be able to use it, in our private and professional lives, during the Pandemic. She wanted the training to use, with her medication resistant patients.

In my practice since opening in 2023 are the following clients or case studies:

Case Study 1 "Belinda L" Female, Canadian Lawyer - weightloss

Articulate mature female Canadian Lawyer had an initial 15-minute free consultation to see if I could help her with weightloss.

During the initial intake questioning, my client advised she felt it all had to do with her wonderful experiences with food when she was a child. She felt she was a happy comfort or emotional eater. Upon further investigation, I also discovered she was currently struggling with a serious medical issue of unmanageable type 2 diabetes, even though she was medically being treated for it. I was able to then establish with her, around the time this autoimmune issue started being out of control, which was recently, which was also when she experienced a painful breakup with her second long-term partner.

Through clinical hypnosis, we Initially regressed back to some wonderful loving times when she, as a young child, would love to visit her Grandmother and her home cooked pies. She believed this is what made her a comfort eater. It always made her feel good anytime of the day or night. Especially apple pies. She had them stored in her freezer. She ate at least two large family size apple pies a week.

In my experience and with my knowledge from College, I probed a little further in one of her regressions with some specific questions and that is when we discovered that Belinda was actually, predominantly, an angry stress eater. We also established she was not comforting herself, she was actually punishing herself, for not speaking up or showing her anger after painful incidents that happened to her. So it wasn't the comfort she was seeking, it was the punishment she felt she needed, to stop herself from verbalising her anger. She was essentially using food to push her emotions and words, down, deep down, inside her and her body was suffering because of it. Belinda was carrying a lot of hurt, fear and anger inside and being a lawyer type she would only articulate logically and not emotionally. This is the way she had trained her brain to function, to be a contracts lawyer. We worked on her inner pain by having her express verbally past emotional hurts and wounds that were triggering the cortisol being released in her system. I also recommended a daily meditation, specifically unique to her, using her words, to help her start her day out right and to create a mindset to stop the compulsive apple pie eating. Belinda later that week reported to only eating half a pie for the whole week compared to her usual two. A month later, she expressed her joy, at being told she was Wonderful everytime she listened to her meditations, which was the start of the day and at night before sleep and that no one had ever called her Wonderful before in her life. I am happy to say Belinda also reported her bgl's had stabilised, she was losing weight and she had given up her pies. She gave the remaining ones away to a neighbour. She felt nothing when she looked at those apple pies now. I used a combination of CBT (cognitive behavioural therapy) and NLP (neuro linguistic programing), psychotherapy and finally, clinical or self hypnosis for Belinda's treatment.

Case study 2. "Barry W" Return Soldier, now Police Officer presenting with Depression.

Trigger Suicide Warning: if you or someone you know are in need of urgent assistance please contact your nearest suicide helpline in your country if you are in Australia please call Lifeline on 13 11 14

Initial free 15-minute consultation, Barry expressed that he felt no one could help him. He complained of headaches, throat tightness and pain. During our initial discussion I discovered he was raised by his single mother. His single Mother always told him, though she loved him, he was a difficult child. He was being raised along with his brilliant first born brother (who went to college) and his sickly younger sister. His father was not physically and emotionally ever in his life. He hated his Father for leaving when he was a young child. He felt his first born Brother had tried to step into the Father and husband role in their family. He resented his mother for always favouring or fawning over his brother and sister, he always felt he was invisible and an afterthought in their family daily lives, especially when he joined the army, where he finally felt accepted and part of something bigger than his family and himself. He felt he had a role and life purpose and male role models finally. He went to war. When he returned from active duty, he left the army and went straight into a front line role as a part of a specialised team that were summoned to car crashes mainly. Where his team used the jaws of life to cut victims from vehicles.

At our first session later that week, I proceeded to help Barry review some memories of his past that may be contributing to his current physical symptoms. In the first scene, he had come upon his best friend who had committed suicide. The scene was harrowing, to say the least. I don't wish to disclose anything further, as this may be a suicide trigger.

When he regressed to the second scene, it was again another harrowing event, where he was walking through a dry cold area, during active duty, and he witnessed another soldier seriously wounded with a ied (an improvised explosive device) right near him. Another close friend and a member of his group. Again he hadn't been able to verbalise, in detail, to anyone before this moment, what he had witnessed and where in his body he was storing and feeling his pain and anguish. He advised in his throat, chest, back and basically a headache that could kill several men. I asked if he wanted to continue, he did. I was so in awe of him. We then went to a third scene, he shared how he felt as a little boy and being constantly frightened for his little sister and how she could die and he felt powerless to stop it or do anything about it.

These were all very painful, powerless memories he shared. Again I asked him where he felt this in his body and he advised his chest and throat plus his head. He said it was a big black heavy cloud thing in his throat and chest and all over his head. I asked him if he was ready to let it go, remove it, to have it leave his body? He said he wasn't able too as it was punishing him for not being enough for his family, he felt unseen and unheard. We then gave his big black heavy cloud thing a new role and purpose in his current life. He couldn't decide on Shadow or Shield so we settled on Shadow Shield. Which I told him was perfect. It had a new role and purpose and a new name. He was in control of it now. It's role was to protect him not punish and torture him like it did before.

Straight after the session, he advised that he felt a 9 and a half out of 10 and that was the best therapy he had ever had. He said he had no pains or aches anywhere in his body. When we started he said he felt he wasn't going to be able to endure the whole session without needing to get up and move around. He said he almost forgot about this thought after the session was over. When we spoke previously at the initial intake he advised he felt like a 4 out of 10. He equated this session to years of therapy in one session.

A month later Barry happily reported the headaches, the throat tightness and pain had stopped right after the session, they had not returned.

With Barry I made a unique recording specifically just for him. One that he could play anytime on his phone with his headphones and no one had to know what he was doing. He could take himself off to his car and meditate on this recording or go and sit in the sun and listen to this anytime he needed it. It was especially formulated just for him, with his words.

Case Study 3 "John M" CEO Builder Australian 50+yrs old – issue with panic attacks and anxiety.

Initial consultation revealed this gentleman was suffering from 3 recent panic attacks, one which happened whilst he was driving, on the weekend, with his child in the seat next to him. His wife referred him to me urgently, as he does not believe in taking any medications. I was acquainted with this person outside of the clinic and was surprised at how quiet, yet his sometimes, joking demeanour was hiding a chronically exhausted and panicked person. The last 3 years had been quite traumatic for him. His Father had passed, he feared for his wife and children being adversely affected by Covid and his business was struggling due to supply issues from the pandemic and the current war in Ukraine.

Firstly, with this gentleman we worked on techniques for managing a panic attack. Then I proceeded to teach him a specific breathwork technique to use daily and throughout the day, without anyone noticing he was doing it. That was the urgent work done.

Then I proceeded to hypnotise him to uncover his triggering beliefs that were feeding his catastrophising. He was not keen on letting someone control his mind and I explained I am not a performance hypnotist, who's objective is to make fun of the members of an audience, I explained my role was to make him feel safe and to take away his triggering thoughts and memories. I then showed him how he was in total control of his mind, the whole time, with a simple quick demonstration. He seemed more reassured to proceed.

From this gentleman's session, I was able to create his own unique daily hypnosis and meditation recording, with a healing sound frequency, that he could listen to, as many times as he needed to, during the day and to help counteract or subdue his feeling out of control and catastrophising thinking. I also created a sleep meditation, unique to him, to listen to every night when he was going off to sleep, to help train his brain back into a regular sleep pattern.

I also shared with him some unique breath work, to shut down his vagus system quickly, if he felt his stress levels rising at work, this was a work health and safety issue on a busy building site.

When I spoke to John later that week he was amazed at how great he was feeling, without medications. He said it was a miracle. He hadn't felt like this in forever. He commented that the breath work and panic attack techniques he can use for the rest of his life. John referred a work colleague to me for something similar.

John has experienced lasting change in how he physically operates in his business and private life. John says he now feels free, in his heart, for the first time in his life.

With all my clients I am reminded of a famous medical saying, I was taught at college and that was from 1895 by Dr Henry Maudsley a British Psychiatrist who was quoted *'The Sorrow Which Has No Vent in Tears May Make Other Organs Weep'*

Breath work that has helped my clients that I would like to share with you in this book. This technique will shut down the Vagus System asap:

This exercise is to be completed, breathing through the nose only (mouth sealed):

- Sit and calmly breathe in through your nose for 4 seconds, hold your breath for 7 seconds, then push, slightly forcefully, out through your nose for 8 seconds and repeat at least 3 times or until you have mastered it.

- I have personally used this technique when I was recently almost hit by another vehicle. It helped with the shock. That horrible feeling in my legs of the adrenal release.

- Just remember no one has to know you are doing this technique. Go to somewhere private eg bathroom, car, work, shut the door in your office etc…

Finally, I wish to say, in my 30 plus years of my career, I truly believe that Psychology and Business are both symbiotic relationships. To grow and work effectively you cannot have one without the other.

About the Author

Leanne McVeigh is the founder and owner of The Corporate Therapist, specialising in working with corporate professionals. Leanne is a kind, considerate, efficient and dedicated therapist, practising practical, clinically proven, researched-backed, non-drug-based therapies for lasting change and happiness with online sessions globally. Leanne is also a member of the Royal Society of Medicine, London. An avid researcher in the fields of neuroscience and mind-body health. Leanne spends her spare time walking in nature, antiquing, spending time with her husband and two sons, plus indulging her pets with way too many toys, all whilst living in bright, beautiful sunny Brisbane, Queensland, Australia.

Website: www.thecorporatetherapist.online for a free 15-minute consultation.
Email: welcome@thecorporatetherapist.online
LinkedIn: www.linkedin.com/in/leanne-mcveigh

Sue Moore

Have you been taking your health for granted?

This question and many others flashed through my mind after I woke up panic-stricken from a 5-hour migraine. I was numb down the right-hand side of my body, unable to feel my right foot with hot and cold tingles across my back.

Was it a stroke?
What was wrong with me?
Was my body failing me?

Let's go back in time and join the dots of how I got to this place in my life …

I grew up in England and during school, I hated running with a passion. I remember during a PE class running around the playing field. I did my best to keep up with the other kids, but by the second corner I thought I was going to collapse. I did finish, although I vowed that I would never run again.

In my head I was constantly saying, "Everyone can run faster than me, I'm not good at this, I'm so unfit, I can't do it and I hate running."

Do you have an inner critic that sabotages your every move too?

Growing up I always loved to travel, have fun and adventures, so in 1990 I followed my 'gypsy' instincts and backpacked around Australia. I fell in love with the country and believed I would move there permanently.

When I returned to England I joined a gym and decided to master running. A personal trainer suggested walking first on a treadmill and then slowly starting to run, building up your distance and speed. So that's what I did and how my running journey began.

Eight years later, I was offered a job in Australia, a dream come true. My first application for permanent residency was denied by Australian Immigration. So I appealed with the help of lawyers proving that 'my job was a specialist role that an Australian couldn't do'. This was a visa requirement at the time. I daily visualised living in Australia until it became a reality.

I loved my life in Australia, probably a little too much. To get back on track with my fitness again, I joined a gym with a goal to lose 7 kilos and run a 14km race. This was the furthest I had ever run.

I fell in love with running and focussed on a 'stretch' goal of running a half marathon.

I once thought I can't run
I once thought I wasn't good enough
I once thought I'm so unfit
I once thought ...

Before long, I was at the starting line of my first half marathon. I had turned my back on excuses, and turned a dream into a reality.

After completing several half marathons, I thought about running a marathon. I remembered watching the London Marathon on TV as a child and seeing ordinary people, from all walks of life completing the marathon.

I thought if they can do it so can I

In the same way I visualised living permanently in Australia, I turned the power of my mind towards completing the Melbourne Marathon.

My training had its ups and downs. One Sunday I had to remind myself of my WHY, as it was -0.5c and I was scheduled to run 30km.

I promised myself to stay committed to the training and to get to the Melbourne Marathon start line injury free. So I just kept showing up and putting one foot in front of the other.

When I completed my first half marathon three years earlier, I felt jubilant but needed to recover for at least a week. If you had told me that three years later I would be training for a marathon and running a half marathon distance for 13 weeks in a row, I wouldn't have believed you.

With the 'baby steps approach' from running a minute and gradually increasing it, I was able to make this happen.

The Day that EVERYTHING changed

You know those events that happen in your life and EVERYTHING is turned on its head. Everyone has them. The thing that matters is the meaning you put on them.

A month before the Melbourne Marathon, I developed a sudden pain in my neck that quickly progressed to a migraine.

I took a couple of painkillers, and went straight to bed. I spent the next five hours attempting to sleep, instead I shivered and groaned. The neighbour's cat stayed with me the whole time just purring and sleeping, as if to reassure me that *'all is well and this soon shall pass.'*

I woke up with numbness in my right foot, a tingling sensation down the right-hand side of my body, my back was burning, and my left hand was difficult to control when I wrote.

I was scared, desolate and panic-stricken. Was it a stroke or worse? What was going on with my body? I just wanted to understand, be better and run again. But my body had other plans …

My doctor recommended that I have a MRI brain scan with the tests back the following week. I thought "If the results were ok I'd run the marathon in 2 weeks' time."

The MRI brain scan showed an 'abnormality' and as the evidence and symptoms weren't conclusive, I had to have more blood tests and a full MRI spine scan.

I was recommended not to run the marathon. Four months of training for nothing. I was devastated.

I was so low in energy that walking upstairs was exhausting so running a marathon was out of the question. I had taken my body for granted all these years expecting it to function, and when it didn't function in a way I was used to, I started to sit up, take notice and listen.

Everything happens for a reason, even if at the time it doesn't make sense

I will never forget the day ... Thursday 20th November 2014, the neurologist told me that the MRI scans showed 8 lesions (inflammation spots) on the brain.

Then it came ... like a right uppercut to your jaw when you're least expecting it.

"And because of the number of lesions you have, the diagnosis is MS."

"I'm the fittest I've been in my life, training for my first marathon, and now you tell me that my body is breaking down and I have MS, multiple sclerosis!" I thought.

MS is a condition where your nerve cells attack your immune system. The communication between the brain, the spinal cord and other parts of the body short circuits.

The shock set in, maybe it was a bad dream that I'd wake up from.

No, THIS was actually happening, this was REAL.
I was told by the neurologist that MS is an incurable disease and that there are medications that may help to prevent the probability of more future attacks happening. If an attack did happen in the future, the medications might help prevent permanent damage leading to disability. As MS is very

individual, they couldn't predict what might happen in the future.

On hearing this I thought "I may or may not have another attack again, and the medication may or may not prevent further attacks from happening. If an attack should happen in the future, the medication may or may not prevent permanent damage. There seems to be a lot of maybes there. That's before you look at the side effects of the recommended medication!"

This didn't make sense to me, so I sought out an alternative. I received a copy of my scans - Point A, my starting point. Now I had to get to point B - fit and well.

I had ignored all the signs and lessons in my life until that point. I had to wait for my 'wake up' call until I stopped, listened to my body and changed my life. I find that most of my clients ignore the signs in their life too. Can you relate?

I had heard stories of people having massive tumours, and worked on their mindset, cleaned up their diet and visualised being healthy. So that's what I would do. I was determined that by my next scan I would have no lesions.

I didn't know how, I just knew that if it was possible for someone else, it was possible for me too.

Before Roger Bannister broke the 4-minute mile, everyone thought it was impossible. Since he broke the record other people instead of believing it's *impossible* they believed *I'M POSSIBLE* and ran a mile in under 4 minutes.

Instead of focusing on negative news, I researched how other people who had been diagnosed with MS had recovered or had adjusted with a renewed quality of life.

I discovered The Institute of Noetic Sciences study on thousands of people who had spontaneous remissions from incurable diseases like cancer and autoimmune diseases.

I read about Annette Fredskov who ran a marathon every day for a year, after receiving an MS diagnosis 2 years earlier, and Kayla Montgomery despite being diagnosed with multiple sclerosis, became one of the best young distance runners in America.

I discovered other people who had received a diagnosis of an incurable disease and were thriving in life after they changed their diet, meditated, reduced stress, overcame their blocked emotions, limiting thoughts and beliefs through kinesiology and mindset work.

Voices of Impact

> "The power that made the body,
> heals the body"
>
> ~ Dr Joe Dispenza

Inspired by all these people, I developed a holistic approach to start 'changing myself from the inside out,' which I now share with my clients.

I slowly retrained myself to run again and three months after the initial diagnosis, I ran 10km pain-free. My new vision during my meditations was to run the Gold Coast Marathon and to have zero lesions in my body.

I believe you too can overcome any adversity in your life and free yourself from all the 'imaginary' boundaries you place on yourself.

Start seeing your perceived 'problems' as opportunities asking yourself what you can learn and what you're grateful for.

In the work I do with my clients, we follow a step-by-step approach which helps them overcome their limitations so that they can achieve their health and lifestyle goals.

I discovered through studying neuroplasticity and quantum

physics that everything is energy and that our thoughts and emotions have a powerful effect on our physical bodies and the results in our lives.

Looking back on my life, I realised that I was my worst critic and my inner dialogue was actually 'attacking' my insides resulting in my body being out of balance, breaking down and creating dis-ease. I find this is a similar pattern with the women I work with too.

It was time for a new identity. It was time to be the best version of myself every single day.

So my plan until my next MRI scan was to work WITH my body, to stay aligned, reduce stress, anxiety and fear from my life. During my daily meditations, I visualised having a healthy brain and believed that by my next neurologist meeting, ALL lesions would be gone.

I made a choice to become consciously aware of my emotions, thoughts and beliefs. I chose to listen to my body when it was out of balance, eat what it needed, seeing FOOD as FUEL providing me with energy.

I chose to be grateful for my life, being present instead of living in the past or the future.

I believe anything is possible if you really want it badly enough. You just have to have a big enough WHY!!!

I gradually built up my running again until I was at the starting line of the Gold Coast Marathon, reflecting back on the journey I had since the MS diagnosis nine months earlier.

I had a dream, broke it down, drew up a plan and took action. I focused on what I had to do each week and kept the big picture in mind.

I believe the MS diagnosis was a gift, a second chance at life. I needed this 'wake-up call' in order to grow and live my life at the next level. I've learnt to listen to my intuition as it always sets me on the 'right' path when I trust and follow it.

The gun went off.

I chatted with Steve, the 4:30 pace setter, who asked about my journey to get to this marathon. I shared with him the last 9 months.

"Good on you for turning it around, being positive and making a go of it, as well as inspiring others. Most people would use that as an excuse to QUIT to give up, not you… good on you Sue," he replied.

A girl in front of us overheard our conversation and said she was diagnosed with MS thirteen years ago and is still running - YAY. Love it.

> "She believed she could, so she did"
> ~ R. S. Grey

One km started to roll into the next and it wasn't long before I was approaching the 21km mark. I started to feel the heat at 30 km as I knew the most, I'd run was 35km. I had to dig deep.

"Just another 5km, then you can walk for a bit. Keep putting one foot in front of the other and you'll make it," I told myself.

Breaking it down into 5km stretches, I was getting closer to the finish line.

3km to go, 1 km to go, and my spirits lifted again. It was hard to stay focused, as tears were welling up in my eyes with a lump in my throat.

I saw the sign "250 metres to go", and I smiled. With my hands in the air, I crossed the finish line.

I Did It!

I visualised the finish line and how I'd feel when I crossed it, months before, I just had to make it happen!

Anything is possible. Just keep putting one foot in front of the other

One month after the marathon I returned to the neurologist who looked at my MRI scans and said, "Out of the eight lesions that showed up in your last scan nine months ago, most of them have completely disappeared and the couple that remain have significantly diminished."

This exact scene I created in my mind, experienced it with all my senses and repeatedly mentally rehearsed it during my daily meditations for the past nine months until it became my 'actual' reality.

Neuroplasticity tells us that your mind doesn't know the difference between an imagined or real event, to your mind it's the same.

Through changing my diet, removing stress from my life, moving to a warmer climate, meditating daily, creating a new identity, addressing blocked emotions, limited thoughts, beliefs and behaviours, I was able to create a new life.

Thank you to my mind, body and soul for changing from the inside out.

I hope my journey has inspired you to follow your own dreams, no matter how big or small they are. Here is my 7-step formula for making it happen.

CREATE - 7 Steps to Making It Happen

1. Belief

Anything is truly possible if you 100% believe it is. If you look back on your life, you made certain things happen because you believed you could.

> "Whether you think you can or you think you can't you're right"
> ~Henry Ford

So, decide NOW that you will commit to making your intention a reality.

2. Vision

Create a vision for yourself that stretches you outside your comfort zone and visualise it daily.

3. Plan

Create a plan for achieving your goal and take daily aligned action.

4. Act As If

- Who do you have to become to have already achieved your goal?

- What strengths and attributes do this person have?

E.g. During my marathon training, I knew the importance of 'sprint training' although it wasn't easy for me. Every week I went to the local athletic track and imagined that I was an elite athlete doing their track sprint sessions.

At first it felt REALLY uncomfortable, but I stuck with it. Within weeks I started to enjoy these sessions, my speed improved as a result of taking consistent action.

5. Track and Tweak

Monitor your emotions, thoughts, beliefs, actions and results against your plan. Adjust anything that's not working and do more of what is working.

6. Celebrate

Reflect and celebrate your results on a weekly basis. This will help you to build momentum and keep going.

7. Rinse and Repeat

Keep repeating steps 1 - 6 until you make it happen

If you want more information on the CREATE method, you can download the free video series here - https://suemoore.online.com/create

Joey, one of my clients followed this method too.

"I have been on a 10-year journey of finding answers to heal my body. Through working with Sue, I created a future as someone who was completely healthy. One of the visions I had was to more than double my income - I had no attachment to how this would happen. I achieved this goal within 4-5 weeks. My health keeps improving even while I am working more. My husband has his wife back after nearly 10 years. A dream come true!"

Your time is now and you're ready for the next step.

Now I'm committed to inspire, educate and empower at least 1,000 women to heal their past traumas so that they can create and live the life they love.

I believe you picked up this book for a reason, and that there are no accidents in life. So, my wish for you is that by sharing my journey with you, it inspires you to live your life fully.

No matter where you're starting from, whatever challenges you've faced or are facing, remember that you are bigger than your setbacks.

You can make your life count, follow your heart and make your dreams a reality.

I believe in you

Sue xo

About the Author

Sue Moore is the founder of Inside Out International and Sue Moore Online. She specialises in a holistic approach to health to achieve transformational results. Born in England, now residing in Queensland, Australia, she is a Health and Wellness Transformational Results Coach, Speaker and Author.

Having studied and worked in the field of neuroscience, mind-body connection and personal transformation for 10 years, Sue specialises in helping people globally master their mindset, follow their heart and maximise their true potential. Featured on Gaia and interviewed on many podcasts, Sue's own health journey and her current work has inspired others to take a holistic approach to their health and life. As a recently qualified Yoga teacher, Sue loves to teach people the benefits of yoga and meditation. When she's not coaching or teaching you will find her at the beach, walking in nature, socialising with family and friends or creating healthy meals.

Email: contact@suemoore.online
Website: https://suemoore.online.com
Instagram: www.instagram.com/suemooreonline

Lara Odushegun

Your current reality... is the reflection of your past!

A few years ago, this statement would have triggered me.

I'd always been a good girl - trying to please everyone, sticking to the rules, dotting my I's and crossing my T's. So why was my life such a mess? What could I have possibly done in my past for me to deserve a reality in which I felt so unhappy?

Perhaps the statement triggers you too?

But the truth of the matter is ... our current reality **IS** the reflection of our past!

The reality you are living in right now is a result of all the thoughts, emotions, and beliefs that you've held onto - and as a result - all the decisions you've made and all the actions you've taken, **until this point.**

Ultimately, it means that **YOU** are responsible for the reality that you are seeing right now because **YOU** are the one that has written your story so far.

I want you to just take a moment to think about what your current reality is.

Do you love what you see? Are you fulfilled? Are you playing at your highest potential?

If you answered no to any of these questions, then I want to encourage you that at any point in time, if you do not like what you see in your current reality, you can choose to create a more fulfilling chapter where you are fulfilled and playing at your highest potential.

On the other hand, if you are happy with your current reality, you may know deep down that you are meant for more and that you are ready to take things to the next level. If this is true, then I also want to encourage you that you can create an even more compelling chapter in your life.

The amazing thing is that... you can **choose** to either be **triggered** by the statement or to be **activated** by it. The fact that your current reality is a **reflection** of your past... means that...it's just a **shadow** of the past... which means that **you** can begin to change it!

You can choose to create a new reality – a new chapter in your life.

"Your past does not equal your future…unless you live there"

- Tony Robbins

But it all begins with a decision.

Growing up, I was a confident child. I was happy, friendly, bubbly, curious … and confident.

But somewhere along the line… I lost that confidence.

Now I can't sit here and tell you that this is exactly the time that I lost my confidence… or this is exactly where I lost it; but fast forward to my young adult self… it was gone. Every now and then, it would pop back up in short bursts… but most of the time, it just wasn't anywhere to be found.

That became my new identity for myself. And I hated it. I hated that I was always self-conscious. I hated that I always doubted myself. I hated that I was never showing up how I wanted to show up. I hated that I wasn't confident like some of the other girls. This was reflected in my thoughts about myself and ultimately my emotions, my beliefs, my decisions, and my actions. I just didn't like myself.

On top of that... I felt like a fraud.

Because on the outside... it seemed that everything was fine...

I had graduated as a Biomedical Scientist. I later decided that I didn't want to spend my lifetime in that field and moved into the IT industry. I worked in the industry for many years and very quickly moved up the ladder.

In one of my roles as a Programmer, I was promoted to Team Leader after 6 months and less than two years in the company I was the Development Manager.

But the thing is I still felt like a fraud.

At work I was this hardworking woman who always got results, but I felt like an imposter. I felt like I wasn't good enough to be in the role and I always felt like one day I would be found out for not really being good enough.

My family always still referred to me as the "confident" one.... So again, I felt like a fraud – because on the inside I did not feel confident at all.

On top of that I felt this sense of not belonging. I was raised in a family where my dad wasn't around; I went to numerous schools growing up; and some of my friends called me a coconut.

I was lacking confidence in myself and more importantly, I was lacking love for myself. When I looked in the mirror… quite frankly… I didn't like what I saw.

But the thing is I felt that if I didn't love myself, it didn't matter because I could find that love from someone else. All I had to do was give them love and shower them with love and they would love me – for me. This gave me a sense of hope. I got married with these expectations. I had a vision of what life should be like. But that wasn't the case.

I was in an unhappy and toxic marriage. I was a sad mess. I felt even more like I didn't belong. I felt lost, unfulfilled, helpless and I felt stuck.

I felt powerless and unlike now, I didn't even know what my purpose was. I had now lost a deeper sense of my identity and who I really was!

Have you ever had a moment like that before, when you've felt lost, stuck, or helpless – or even powerless – like you'd given your power away?

That's how I felt, and I realised that I **had** given my power away. But even with that realisation, I was too scared to break free. I was scared of stepping outside of my comfort zone. I was scared of the unknown. I was scared of starting over. And on top of that I was ashamed of what other people would say. So, I stayed.

On the surface – I was in a good marriage. I had a successful career… underneath… I was a mess! My self-doubt increased, my self-worth decreased, and I continued to feel like an imposter, yet still I stayed – thinking that things might get better. But things did not get better.

I remember one day – I came to the sudden awareness of how unhappy I was. I was so unhappy – and in that moment, I knew that I couldn't ignore it anymore. I knew that I DID NOT WANT TO FEEL THIS WAY ANYMORE. I thought there must be more to life than this, and when the pain of staying became more unbearable than the fear of the unknown or the fear of starting over… I knew I had to break free.

That's when I made the decision that it was time to take back my power… and it was time to remember who I truly was.

It was hard… and at first, I doubted my decision. But I discovered that the first step in remembering who you are is learning to love yourself; and the first steps in learning to love yourself; is learning to listen and trust yourself.

So, I decided to trust myself and trust my decision. I had to take control of my own life... I had to learn to love myself; and that love had to come from within – not from the outside.

And the thing is... once I made that decision... I felt this sense of freedom... this sense of just feeling free. It was as if I'd been carrying this weight (that I didn't even know I'd been carrying) and now I'd let go of it – and I could breathe.

BUT with that new sense of freedom... was also fear. The fear of not knowing what was going to happen next. I found myself in a place where I was asking myself, "Now what?" I'd been married for 13 years. I'd been writing the same chapter over and over again. It was all I knew. The pages were all too familiar to me. The thought of turning the page over to a blank page – to rewrite a new story, scared the hell out of me.

But the truth is, it is never too late to rewrite your story – turn a new page and start a new chapter.

I started working on myself. I read many books; and did a lot of courses. I did daily inner work. I worked on my mindset. I worked on my identity. I worked on my self-image.

I created and implemented daily routines that incorporated new habits and techniques. And by implementing this daily routine I learned to embrace who I am, and I was able to start seeing on the outside... who I truly wanted to be.

I trusted the process. I was consistent and here I am today back into my power and loving me ☺

Now I help other women who doubt their worth and are feeling stuck and unfulfilled in their life. I help them go from self-doubt to self-worth so that they are able to step into their true power; to create the life they want (and deserve). I share with them the strategies that I used to regain my power; love myself unapologetically; and become the more confident me.

Working on my self-image was a very important part of the process. This helped me to see myself in a healthier and more accurate way. It helped me learn to love myself on the inside and learn to love what I saw when I looked in the mirror. I have shared these tips with my clients and it has helped them to develop a positive self-image.

Here are 3 tips I would love to share with you:

1. Reflect on your personal strengths and accomplishments
Take time to think about your personal strengths and the things you have accomplished - and make a list of them. Reflect on how these strengths and accomplishments have positively impacted your life and the lives of those around you.

2. Keep a daily gratitude journal
Take a few minutes to write down things you are grateful for about yourself. Reflecting on the positive aspects of yourself can help shift your focus away from negative thoughts and emotions.

3. Practice positive self-talk.
By engaging in positive self-talk, you can learn to challenge and overcome any negative thoughts and cultivate a more positive outlook. You can also focus on positive affirmations.

These tips helped me and have helped my clients. I hope that it will help you too. You can visit my *website* to download a free PDF on tips to Improve Your Self-Talk as well as more tips to Develop a Positive Self-Image.

I re-discovered my passion; I found my voice; I found myself; and in the process, I remembered why I'm here and what my purpose is… to teach self-love; to help women go from self-doubt to self-worth and help them remember who they truly are. I help them to create a new pathway so that they can have more freedom and fulfilling experiences. My signature system helps my clients to create the next chapter of their life with clarity, confidence and conviction. My nine-step framework takes my clients from self-doubt to self-worth and has different processes including those that help them to create empowering beliefs and heal any trauma from their past. They feel more empowered, more courageous and more capable in themselves and their abilities. This leads to them taking aligned action towards their goals and desires.

For example, one of my clients – an aspiring Writer, came to me because she was struggling with limiting beliefs that was holding her back from progressing and taking action. Having taken a break from writing she was struggling from a lack of self-belief. She believed that no one would want to read her blog. She struggled with imposter syndrome and questioned her abilities as a writer. Her reactive states and patterns had led to feelings of frustration and debilitation and the actions that she was taking to work through them wasn't successful. It wasn't how she wanted to live her life, so she reached out to me. Before her session with me, she felt heavy with self-doubt and insecurities. After one session of Timeline Therapy, we were able to heal the deeply rooted fears and emotions - freeing her from the limiting beliefs. Her negative emotions were dissolved, and she felt a sense of LIGHTNESS. She felt RENEWED, REENERGISED, POWERFUL and CAPABLE... and she felt inspired and courageous to start writing again.

Since I started coaching, my own personal development has not stopped. I realised that even a coach needs a coach! I have since worked with many coaches; and invested money in many programmes and invested in myself. I am a firm believer in lifelong learning. I believe that self-development and growth is an ongoing process. It's all about the Long Time Horizon. I continue to invest in myself because I believe that the more I up-level myself – the better I can serve and support my clients. So, I continue to share all that I have learned with my clients – and use the life changing tools and techniques to help them to transform their life and become the best versions of themselves.

I am committed to the journey of self, and this means that I am constantly choosing to step outside of my comfort zone repeatedly. When I first started coaching, I didn't want to put myself out there. But there came a point when I realised that if I wanted to make more impact, I would have to put myself out there and be more visible. This brought up a lot of fear in me.

For a long time, I had learned to be comfortable blending in and not standing out. For a long time, I had felt like my voice didn't matter and that I did not have anything important to say. Who would want to listen to me?! The thought of putting myself out there and the thought of being visible felt very scary. But I have learnt as one of my mentors told me - that my conviction must be stronger than my convenience. So, every time it's time to step outside of my comfort zone again, I choose to lean into the fear, dance with it and keep taking steps towards my mission. The thing is…every time you take a small step forward, what you find is that like with any muscle that you work, it becomes stronger.

In choosing to show up for myself, I'm also choosing to show up for my clients! I want them to feel empowered that they too have a voice and can stand in their power – knowing who they are. They no longer need to hide. They deserve to be visible and have their voice heard – because their voice matters.

For example, one of my clients – a Transformational Coach, came to me because she was struggling to get clients. She wanted to share her gift with the world but at the same time she feared judgement; and she was scared to put herself out there and be visible. This meant that although she wanted to grow her coaching business – instead she kept choosing to stay small. This left her feeling frustrated. When she came to me – she was in a very low place, feeling overwhelmed, stuck in pain and procrastination; and not able to move forward.

Taking her through the program, she was able to remember and rediscover who she truly was. She connected to her bolder self, and I was able to guide her to fully embody this bolder self. She gained more confidence and strength and was able to take more actions. She was able to put herself out there which was a bold move for her. This ultimately led to her getting her first client. She was able to experience progress each day and continue to build momentum. After the program she felt more empowered; a greater love for herself and told me that she felt that she had become a greater version of herself.

I have had the privilege of working with many women from various countries to help them overcome their limiting beliefs. My mission now is to help as many women around the world as I can - go from self-doubt to self-worth; become the best versions of themselves, and fully step into their true power. To do this I will be creating more online programs and workshops. I will also be speaking at more global events – so that, on a global scale – I can help more women remember who they truly are.

You see when you've forgotten who you are; you've done what the world expects; you've followed the rules of the world…and you've not been true to you… your soul begins to scream, "No! Now it's my turn!" And that's when you know that it's time to come back into the relationship with yourself and what you were meant to do on this planet.

What you're doing right now will shape your future. With every new moment comes an opportunity for a fresh start. Are you ready to create the next chapter? Are you ready to step out of the life you are currently living and create the life you really want – intentionally?

No more excuses. It's your time to shine.

Follow me on my Facebook page *@lara.odushegun* for more tips and resources to help you go from self-doubt to self-worth and how to create the next chapter of your life with clarity, confidence and conviction. Remember, **Love YOU first** ♥

About the Author

Lara Odushegun is the founder of Sow Success – a platform that encourages people to define their own meaning of success and then sow seeds of this success each and every day. She is a Self-Love and Empowerment Coach and is passionate about empowering people to find the power within to create the life they want. Lara helps women go from self-doubt to self-worth to create the next chapter of their life with clarity, confidence and conviction. She has inspired, and helped to change the lives of hundreds of women around the world and has been featured on global platforms online. Lara is from the United Kingdom and enjoys spending time with her two children. She loves music and enjoys dancing, singing, and writing songs. She often shares words of inspiration through short songs on her Facebook page. She also loves travelling and meeting people.

Email: lara@sowsuccess.co.uk
Facebook: www.facebook.com/lara.odushegun
Website: www.sowsuccess.co.uk

Kerstin Rheinlander

TRAVEL has always been a major part of my life. My eyes light up given the chance to talk about travel, to share my experiences and to simply inspire others to find out what the world has to offer. From a very early age I felt drawn to go out, explore and connect with people. My first attempts at networking were at the age of four knocking on people's doors with my little spiel" Hi, my name is Kerstin, can I come in for a cookie?" The neighbourhood lovingly called me the "cookie girl" with daily anticipation who I would visit next. In the late 60s this was still safe, I don't think I would recommend this approach today. My trusted steed at that time was my tricycle which took me across major streets and intersections creating some angst for my parents but oh so much joy for me. But slowly I evolved to use bigger and faster modes of transport to take me to new destinations. It was a mystery to my parents where I had caught this travel bug and with that the constant urge to go to new places and meet new people, as if I was on a mission searching for something.

My parents weren't travel people, nevertheless they supported my desire to explore the big wide world. Initially, it was to attend language exchange programs in the UK and the USA to improve my English (I was born and raised in Germany). Rebelling against my parents wish to embark on a banking career (this would have been my worst nightmare!) I booked myself a one-way train ticket to Paris and found work as an Au-pair, to learn the language and enjoy the French Savoir Faire – yes, I had my "Emily in Paris" moment and loved every minute of it. Fluent in French as well as English, I was accepted as a trilingual flight attendant with Lufthansa German Airlines. I could not have landed a better job to feed my travel bug, and even better, the company paid me to travel, travel & travel more. I visited every continent, except the Arctics, multiple times and had plenty of on the ground time to learn about other cultures, traditions, food, languages and local ways of life. Through all this travel I realised that I had some natural abilities: excellent customer service skill, empathy and compassion as well as the drive to find solutions to improve or make someone's day or experience a lot better.

Long-haul night flights and constant jetlag took a toll on my wellbeing and sleep patterns, so I grounded myself to find more balance and try something new (always on the lookout for the next adventure). But true to my style it had to be different. Hong Kong seemed liked a great place to live, a great base for more in-depth Asia exploration, so I packed my bags and moved from a small German town to the Asian metropolis. As it happened someone, a handsome single man, was looking for a 1st mate/deck hand on a 55ft yacht – why not, right? A bit of adventure on a floating "home" sounded like fun. It was for a while, but the love story ended with betrayal, a broken heart and some ugly legal matters. Lessons learnt and trust in men destroyed for a while my determination kicked in to thrive in a city, which at that time was considered the most expensive in the world. My knowledge of travel and customer services soon landed me a job looking after a CEO and his corporate travellers, followed by the best job ever: Senior Sales Executive for all the VIP travellers of the local Lufthansa branch – dream job No2.

Living in Hongkong I observed that Chinese people placed a lots of emphasis on healthy living, so I embraced Chinese medicine, Tai Chi and other remedies to improve my overall wellbeing, focus only on me, no men!

Don't you just love it when the universe throws you a curveball? Just as I was enjoying my best life the universe delivered the perfect man - kind, gentle, open-minded and an avid traveller too. Marriage followed, relocation to the US and lots of travel exploring the land of possibilities. Child 1 arrived shortly after with Child No2 completing the family. Child No 2, however, was the challenge child due to health issues which led to post-natal depression and extreme sleep deprivation as Child No2 did not sleep for 18 month - not a pretty combo. With the help of friends as I had no family to turn to, I managed to pull myself out of the dark zone using yoga and meditation, again trying to focus as much as possible on my wellbeing so I could be the best mum for my children.

After Asia and US, we somehow had become restless, the US was certainly not our forever home, there had to be a better place. Again, the seeker in me reared its head to continue the search for my perfect place in the world.

Welcome to Australia – I found my forever home!

I will not lie, initially it was hard to put down roots, even though I was in my happy place, but at the same time I felt completely lost and in total culture shock. Once more the universe helped and put the right people in front of me to assist and guide me. I connected with a school mum who happened to be a home-based travel agent. She pulled me back into the fold of the travel world, this time as a retail travel agent. I was not only coming home to "my country" but also coming home to "my world of travel". With her help I established my own business and build my client base from scratch. My efforts saw my travel business grow but without clarity on my ideal client, my business failed as I attracted people that were not aligned with me, not to mention the mental stress and the sleepless nights which were all caused due to lack of boundaries. This took a toll on my family, my marriage and myself. I had vowed to never slip into depression mode again, so I walked away from my business and it felt as if a weight was lifted off my shoulders. Do not get me wrong, I am not a quitter but selfcare was my priority.

The months that followed I embarked on a creative healing journey and completed training as an Artbundance Coach. I painted and worked with colour and other materials every day for 60 days straight. This resulted in so many "Aha" moments and epiphanies while creating with my hands. I discovered a side of me that I did not know. Remember I had mentioned customer service and problem solving? I have since added intuition to the skills set. I just have this knowing to listen, hold the space and intuitively ask the right questions that help people explore their feelings and find their own answers. Who knew? As I was not confident enough to really use this newfound skill, guess what happened? I ended up in the travel industry – it is like an addiction. Let's just stick with what is comfortable, right? Back to what I knew with the difference I was working for others meant that as soon as I walked out of the office the day was done. I sold a lot of travel, built new connections and earned great commissions but it bugged me that someone else was benefitting from my efforts. This did not sit right with me. Miss Independence was shining through again.

The time had come to use my evolved skills, rebuild and run my own business, again. Round 2, but this time I applied all the new skills, found the right clients, set boundaries and slowly but steadily build a thriving travel business that I was proud of. I was rewarded with many travel opportunities and loved, loved, loved it! I was back in my element and aligned with my true purpose.

And then COVID happened.

Literally overnight the rug was pulled out from underneath me and my business that I had carefully curated was destroyed/decimated or whatever you want to call it. Border closures meant that I no longer had a business. Every trip I had booked over 18 months was cancelled. Income I had earned and paid taxes on was recalled, and I had become liable to refund thousands of dollars. It was not as simple as cancelling and refunding customers, as monies were sitting overseas with suppliers or airlines. The whole industry was an unfathomable mess, and no one knew how to handle this new situation of reverse engineering billions of dollars of travel bookings worldwide. "Unprecedented" was the word used repeatedly to make sense of the situation that seemed like the longest deep dive ever. I looked after my clients to the best of my ability, however in a crisis the true nature of some clients emerged who attacked me, threatened me, called me names, pursued me with legal action and so much more. I worked day and night with lack of sleep pushing me to the brink of collapse and exhaustion. Wine, Vodka and chocolate consumption were in excess, not healthy at all, but a coping tool at that time to numb my feeling of loss and despair. The emotions were at an all-time high with huge financial losses, no clear direction and no outlook, nothing to even hold on to for a little glimpse of hope. My family was my only solace at that time. Every day I felt like standing on the edge of an abyss, with only darkness ahead. Eventually the government offered Job Keeper, a short-lived Woohoo, which enabled me to refund my clients bit by bit, however it was not enough.

A friend, so I thought at the time, offered me a casual job which I gratefully accepted, just to add some funds which ultimately went to clients in any case. In the midst of sorting my mess, this friend betrayed me by cancelling out my government support payment to benefit her company, for which she was not even entitled too. Another ugly mess I did not need. Until this point, I had handled negativity and hardship within the travel industry as well as the loss of my business like a fighter, but this betrayal was the final blow and pushed me over the edge. I fell in a heap and all the emotions accumulated over the previous four months poured out of me. I cried for days curled up in a corner. Anytime my husband or anyone tried to talk to me I burst into tears. If this is what it felt like to have your back against the wall, well then, I had hit rock bottom and did not see a way out of this dark and desperate space.

For the first time in my life, I knew I needed professional help. It took all my strength to make that phone call. As soon as this friendly voice answered the phone, the floodgates of tears opened again.

Within 10 minutes, I had a psychologist on the line and after an hour he managed to give me a lifeline and some tools to manage my day. Many more sessions followed to help me find ways to cope and see possibilities again. How do you recover from such a blow?

I really had no clue where to start but my intuition knew I needed to make myself a priority. So, I started walking 2-3 hours a day, first on my own listening to motivational books and once I was ready to connect again a friend joined me who had also suffered and was trying to make sense of "What next?". We walked every day and we talked. We shared our deepest feelings, angsts and worries. It was raw and vulnerable but at that time we both needed these walks/talks.

As it happened I came across a course as Wellness Travel Specialist (travel again – I must be crazy!) but the content intrigued me and I instinctively knew that wellness would become more prominent in the months to come as many people were suffering. It was just what I needed as a new focus, or to use the word of the moment "a pivot". The course was not so much about selling wellness travel but rather understanding the elements of wellness and what wellness travel really means and its benefits.

As part of the course all participants were challenged to test one of the wellness modalities – I choose the ancient Indian practice of Ayurveda meaning "Science of Life". I booked myself a consultation with an Ayurvedic doctor and followed the prescription of Ayurvedic herbs and massages as well as breathing exercises and daily movement. Determined to make a point, I applied these principles religiously. As a result, I lost weight, slept better, gained more energy, increased my happiness and felt like a new person. Wow! - this was powerful. I have since adopted some of the practices but also have slipped a little and that is ok.

The story does not end here. Inspired by this experience I returned to a previous course I had completed a few years back on the basics of wellness coaching, it was hobby at that time to guide me through a recovery phase from major surgery, but I now know that this was a path I needed to take. Over 6 months I clamped down, upgraded my studies and finished as a Professional Certified in Health and Wellness Coach. Isn't it amazing what you can achieve if you have direction?

Through my Wellness coaching training I have seen the impact just a few sessions can have on a person's wellbeing and mindset. It does not take a lot to implement little lifestyle change. People always think there needs to be a big shift with a lot of sacrifices but in fact smaller changes consistently applied show longer lasting impact.

With all the personal hardship I have experienced as a business owner and the time I needed to grieve and heal from the destruction of my business, applying the strategies of wellness coaching have literally brought me back to life. I observe women in business struggle under so much pressure, sometimes pushing themselves to prove a point and challenging themselves to be better than their male counterparts. But at what cost? Without self-care women are not any good for their business nor their families, they simply become functioning robots on autopilot with no real spark for life left. Yet, it is so easy to make time to nourish the flame within and let your light shine bright. Now imagine wellness coaching and travel combined. This is match made in heaven and I am about to deliver this.

With the re-opening of the Australian borders in Feb2022 to recommence international travel, my dormant travel business went from hibernation to extreme demand overnight. Back in Feb/Mar2020 I logged 12–14-hour days to unravel all travel arrangements, now I was being inundated with travel requests, once again working long hours to manage huge pent up demand for international travel, particularly to reunite families worldwide. My travel business was catapulted to new heights beyond my wildest imagination. My determination combined with a passion for travel to remain in an industry paid off, even though for the longest time it felt like the light at the end of the tunnel would never shine.

In hindsight, I am grateful for the chance to reset my business, to review processes, restructure and emerge like the "Phoenix from the Ashes" bigger, better and stronger with more clarity. With business elevating to new heights, selfcare was needed not to fall back into utter exhaustion and burnout. Luckily, I now can see the signs and counteract to ensure selfcare is included as part of my success.

Moving forward, now that I have rebuild my travel business, my focus will be on YOU – women in business leading a busy, hectic life who just need a break to disconnect in order to practise selfcare and re-energise. Selfcare does not mean that you need to follow the diet and exercise hype, it means to look after YOU and incorporate what brings YOU joy and lifts YOUR happy vibration. That could be a massage in the morning and cocktails in the evening, it could be a 20km hike in nature followed by a swim in a waterfall, it could be anything YOU want it to be as long as you make it about YOU.

Now that my travel world is back in order, would you come along on such a retreat/escape/timeout where YOU can be YOU with a huge benefit to your overall wellbeing and a way to recharge by disconnecting and maybe connecting with like-minded women?

It is my goal to see you "Shine Through Wellness" in business and life as well as equip you with tools and strategies that you can weather any storm. Remember the airline phrase: "Put on your own mask before your help others", this is exactly what is needed for YOU to thrive and succeed.

I have created some wellness packages that you can enjoy as a solo traveller but am also working on a few group wellbeing escapes to places that nurture and inspire. Are you in? Don't you think YOU owe it to yourself to be the best version of YOU......That is why motto is: Travel = Wellness[3]

It is your time to shine – I would love to be your guide along the way.

About the Author

Kerstin started travelling the world 40 years ago and has worked in various fields of travel for the past 35 years while living on 4 different continents. Her knowledge of the travel industry and passion for creating experiences that last a lifetime has seen her built a successful travel business catering to the discerning and well-travelled client.

As a professional certified health and wellness coach she now combines travel with wellness/wellbeing to coach and encourage women in business to take a break and disconnect from life in order to practice self-care and re-energise. She offers ready-made wellness packages for solo travellers and also annual retreats that nurture and inspire women to be the best version of themselves. She is an advocate for self-care not being a luxury, but a necessity to thrive and shine.

Facebook: @TravelmanagersKerstinRheinlander
Website: www.travelmanagers.com.au/KerstinRheinlander
Email: Kerstin.rheinlander@travelmanagers.com.au

Lauren Rogers

I never dreamed that one day I would become an Artist! I am a proud Australian Ngarabal & Torres Strait Islander woman, a Contemporary Indigenous Artist, and I love sharing my culture and stories through my art! It has been an incredible life of personal learnings while adventuring and exploring this big, beautiful Country of ours, the place I call home, Australia.

Art has always been in my heart! My first clear childhood memories start when I was about five or six years old, always drawing, colouring, or painting. I was a creative kid, constantly experimenting with the arts! I loved sharing my magical view of the world through my artwork! Art has always played a significant role throughout my life.

Reflecting on my childhood, it was a very artistic time making art, painting, singing, dancing, and exploring my creativity! Then I grew up, and art wasn't a big part of my life until recently; it magically came back into my life!

A couple of years ago, I didn't see it at the time, but there was a significant change on the horizon. My Mother never knew her father, so she took a DNA test. After a lifetime of trying to find him, we had hope! The DNA test results returned, revealing that my grandfather was an Aboriginal man, a Ngarabal man with bloodlines to the Torres Strait Islands. Sadly, just as we discovered this life-changing news, we also found that he had passed only years earlier, so as fate would have it, we never got the chance to meet him! The family drew comfort from finding the missing piece of our family puzzle and meeting many relatives we never knew! The family connection ignited a deep curiosity about my culture, stories and family history. As the years passed, I leaned in to learn, yarned and listened to stories from our mob!

One balmy summer afternoon, I remember sitting in the back sunroom, pondering life and feeling the desire to paint again after years of not holding a paintbrush! I drove to the art shop that afternoon to get paint supplies. It was as if a new door had opened that afternoon and dared me to take a new path, one that not in my wildest dreams could have imagined, into the world of art! Something that I always dreamed about as a child.

I started layering paint down on the canvas, wondering what to paint or what direction to take. I took a deep breath and started putting little dots down in a row, then the next row, a twist and turn, and another colour. This painting came together in an extraordinary explosion of a hundred tiny dots, representing the start of my journey back to art, culture and family. I called this piece of art, Coming Home. It was to be my first Contemporary Indigenous art piece.

This art piece propelled me into the beautiful art world again. It has been a precious gift to learn about Aboriginal Australia's history and my Country, Ngarabal Nation. As time passed, I kept painting, learning, researching, meeting Elders, yarning, exploring the family archives and making connections. My eyes opened to our Nation's history, the massacres, dispossessions and marginalisation of Aboriginal and Torres Strait Islander people. The effects of colonialism are still being felt today after 235 years!

I was born in 1983, sixteen years after this Country held a referendum in which Australia voted overwhelmingly to include the Traditional Owners of the land in the census as our First Nations people were not counted in Australia's 1901 Constitution.

I am trying to remember what was taught about First Nations history in school. I remember being taught something about the Dreamtime, then quickly returning to learning about Captain Cook and other white historical figures. I remember this minimising of the non-white history of our Country continued into my high school years. I understand nowadays that schools around Australia have some Aboriginal and Torres Strait Islander teachings included in the curriculum. However, I would like to see more education, honouring the histories of our First Nations people for all our children to learn. This is the start of truth-telling. The truth is that Aboriginal and Torres Strait Islander peoples have lived on this continent for over 65,000 years. Captain Cook did not discover Australia because people were already here, living on the land and thriving!

I discovered that after the ships arrived, massacres broke out, the Frontier Wars, as the white settlers began desecrating the Traditional Owners of the lands. Genocide of Aboriginal and Torres Strait Islander people occurred across the Country, the massacres of Aboriginal people were conducted in secrecy, and few perpetrators were ever brought to justice.

Aboriginal people had little chance of surviving. Their spears, clubs and hatchets had to fight swords, pistols, muskets, double-barrelled shotguns, rifles, carbines, and bayonets, among other items and any survivors from massacres were often enslaved.

I also learned about the Stolen Generations. Since colonisation, numerous government laws, policies and practices resulted in the forced removal of generations of Aboriginal and Torres Strait Islander children from their families and communities across Australia. This was called the assimilation policy under our government at the time. Between 1910 and 1970, many

Indigenous children were taken from their families and 'assimilated' into non-Indigenous homes or placed under State care. These children are known as the Stolen Generations, and many are still searching for their families today. The children were often neglected and abused, their names were changed, and they weren't permitted to honour their culture or speak their language. The hope at the time was for Indigenous Australians to be erased from society or, at the very least, be assimilated into 'white' society.

After some time, the Frontier Wars ended. As the violence subsided, the government put new policies of control and discrimination in place. First Nations people stood in their strength, and on 26 January 1938, an Annual Day of Mourning was declared. This day reflected on the pain and injustice of colonisation and the necessity of continued resistance in defending First Nations people. There is so much to mourn, the loss of land, culture, language and the loss of our Elders who led our struggle in generations past.

These were my first learnings of First Nations' histories in Australia. It is time we do better as a Nation to start truth-telling by acknowledging our past histories and creating a space for reparations. There have been many failed attempts at treaties and reconciliation over the past two centuries. It is time for our First Nations peoples to be included in the Australian Constitution.

We must walk forward together in healing and reconciliation to be the great Nation grounded in the longest-living culture on earth. The invasion that started at Botany Bay is the origin of the fundamental grievance between the old and new Australians and that Australia was colonised without the consent of its rightful owners.

Now there is an opportunity for First Nations people to tell the truth about history and for Australians to hear those voices and reconsider what they know and understand about their Nation's history. This will be challenging, but the truth needs to be told.

Later this year, our Country will go to a referendum to finally decide to acknowledge our Traditional Custodians of the lands into the Constitution. The people have made these calls for recognition since 1846 when Exiled Tasmanian Aboriginal people on Flinders Island petitioned Queen Victoria about the agreement with Colonel Arthur.

In May 2017, over 250 Aboriginal and Torres Strait Islander delegates from all points of the Southern Sky gathered in Mutitjulu in the shadow of Uluru and put their signatures on a historical statement. The Uluru Statement from The Heart addressed the Australian people, inviting the Nation to create a better future. A call for establishing a First Nations Voice to be enshrined in the Constitution.

Voices of Impact

Look deeper into our First Nations' history over the past 235 years. Below, I have highlighted significant events in a timeline of our Australian history so you can see the struggles, the failed attempts at treaty and reconciliation and the constant broken promises from our governments.

1770 – Invasion - Captain James Cook claims the land now known as Australia.

1788 - First Fleet - Captain Arthur Phillip and the First Fleet arrive at Botany Bay.

1846 - Petition Queen Victoria - exiled Tasmanian Aboriginal people on Flinders Island petitioned Queen Victoria about an agreement with Colonel Arthur.

1890-1899 - Debates over a Federal Constitution. Aboriginal people are not involved and barely mentioned in Conventions.

1901 - The Constitution came into force. Australian Parliament consists of two Houses (the Senate and the House of Representatives) and the King, represented in Australia by the Governor General. Aboriginal people continue to be forced onto reserves and missions under racial segregation acts known as 'Protection' legislation.

1933 - Petitioning for representation in Federal Parliament. Yorta Yorta man, William Cooper, petitions the King seeking intervention, including representation in the federal Parliament. The Commonwealth does not send it on to the King. Aboriginal man Joe Anderson, also known as King Burraga, calls for Indigenous representation in the Federal Parliament.

Voices of Impact

1934 - Urge to take over Aboriginal Affairs. David Unaipon urges Commonwealth to take over Aboriginal Affairs from the States.

1937 - Petition for representation in Parliament. Yorta Yorta man William Cooper petitions King George VI for representation in Parliament.

1938 - Day of Mourning. The Australian Aborigines League and the Aborigines Progressive Association hold a 'Day of Mourning' on 26 January, the sesquicentenary of the British colonisation of Australia.

1949 - Australia Aborigines League. Secretary of Australia Aborigines League Doug Nicholls wrote to Prime Minister Chifley seeking representation of Aboriginal people in the Federal Parliament.

1962 - The right to vote. The right to vote in federal elections was extended to all Aboriginal and Torres Strait Islander people.

1967 - Constitutional Referendum. A referendum was held granting the Federal Parliament power over Indigenous affairs and enabling Aboriginal people to be counted as part of the Australian population for constitutional purposes.

1979 - Call for a Treaty. Following nationwide consultations with Aboriginal and Torres Strait Islander communities, the National Aboriginal Conference calls for a treaty to be negotiated between Aboriginal people and the Commonwealth.

1983 - Two hundred years later. Senate Standing Committee on Legal and Constitutional Affairs hands down its report Two Hundred Years Later, which recommends the government consider a treaty in consultation with Aboriginal peoples.

1988 - The Barunga Statement. A second bark petition is presented to Prime Minister Bob Hawke by Yolngu man, Galarrwuy Yunupingu. The Barunga Statement calls for recognition of Aboriginal rights, for a nationally elected Aboriginal and Islander organisation to oversee Aboriginal and Islander affairs, and for the Commonwealth to negotiate a treaty. Prime Minister Bob Hawke commits to a treaty by 1990.

1989 - Establishment of ATSIC. The Federal Parliament creates a new independent statutory body, the Aboriginal and Torres Strait Islander Commission (ATSIC), after an extensive consultation period, including five hundred meetings with 14,500 people.

1991 - Breaking the promise of a treaty, the government proposes a statutory Reconciliation process instead. In breaking the commitment to deliver a treaty, the government says Australians need to be educated more about Indigenous peoples.

1992 - Native Title recognised by the High Court. The High Court delivered judgment in the Mabo case, holding that native title survived the British acquisition of sovereignty.

1993 - Native Title Act passed. The Keating government passes the Native Title Act after months of pressure, protest and tough negotiations. The government also promises a land fund to compensate those whose native title has been extinguished and a social justice package to advance reconciliation.

1995 - Recognition, Rights and Reform Report. ATSIC delivers the Recognition, Rights and Reform Report, which outlines a range of sweeping proposals for the Keating government's social justice package, including constitutional recognition. The social justice package is never implemented.

1997 - Bringing Them Home Report tabled. The Human Rights and Equal Opportunity Commission tables the Bringing Them Home report, which examines the long history of racially discriminatory Australian laws and policies that resulted in the widespread removal of Aboriginal and Torres Strait Islander children from their families. Among its fifty-four recommendations is a call for an official apology from the Commonwealth Government. Prime Minister John Howard refuses to provide this.

2000 - The Roadmap for Reconciliation. The Council for Aboriginal Reconciliation delivers its Australian Declaration towards Reconciliation and the Roadmap for Reconciliation. The report reinforces Aboriginal and Torres Strait Islander aspirations for a treaty and constitutional change.

2005 - Abolition of ATSIC. Parliament formally abolishes ATSIC.

2007 - New commitment to Constitutional Preamble. Shortly before the 2007 election, Prime Minister John Howard announces the government's intention to hold a referendum to symbolically recognise Aboriginal and Torres Strait Islander peoples in a new preamble to the Constitution.

2008 - Apology to the Stolen Generations. Prime Minister Kevin Rudd presents the Apology to the Stolen Generations. The Australia 2020 Summit is held, with the final report noting the 'strong view that recognition of Aboriginal and Torres Strait

Islander peoples' rights needs to be included in the body of the Constitution, not just in the Preamble.

2008 - Yolngu and Bininj Leaders present a Statement of Intent to the Prime Minister. The Prime Minister is presented with a Statement of Intent from Yolngu and Bininj Leaders, who express their desire for constitutional protection of traditional land and cultural rights.

2013 - Recognition Act. With support from the Opposition, the Gillard government passes the Aboriginal and Torres Strait Islander Peoples Recognition Act 2013 to provide an interim form of recognition of Aboriginal people.

2015 - Referendum Council Established. Indigenous Leaders meet with Prime Minister Malcolm Turnbull and Opposition Leader Bill Shorten at Kirribilli House and issue the Kirribilli Statement. In response, the Prime Minister and Opposition Leader establish the Referendum Council.

2016-2017 - First Nations Constitutional Dialogues. The Referendum Council runs thirteen First Nations Regional Dialogues to discuss constitutional reform options and ensure that Aboriginal decision-making is at the Heart of the reform process.

2017 - The Uluru Statement. The Referendum Council holds a National First Nations Constitutional Convention at Uluru to ratify the decision-making of the Regional Dialogues. The Convention delegates draft and overwhelmingly endorse the Uluru Statement from the Heart, issued to the Australian people. This calls for a constitutionally entrenched First Nations Voice to

Parliament and a Makarrata commission to oversee a treaty-making process and truth-telling. The Referendum Council hands down its final report, which endorses the Uluru Statement from the Heart and its call for Voice, Treaty and Truth. The Turnbull Government rejects the call for a Voice in Parliament.

2018 - Recommendation for Co-design. A Joint Select Committee of Parliament to consider the work of the Referendum Council, chaired by Senators Patrick Dodson and Julian Leeser, undertakes its work. Its final report finds that the Voice is the only viable recognition proposal. It recommends the government 'initiate a co-design process [of the Voice] with Aboriginal and Torres Strait Islander peoples.

2019 - Co-Design Process. In the pre-election budget, the government commits $7m to a Voice co-design process and $160m to running a referendum. Then, Minister for Indigenous Australians, Ken Wyatt, announces a 'co-design' process to determine the structure and functions of the Voice. The constitutional enshrinement of the Voice was excluded from the terms of reference.

2021 - Sydney Peace Prize. The interim report on the Indigenous Voice Proposal was released. Stage two of the 'co-design' process commences, inviting feedback on the proposals for the design of the Voice. The Uluru Statement wins the Sydney Peace Prize with co-laureates Pat Anderson, Megan Davis and Noel Pearson.

2022 - Labor Leader Albanese reconfirmed his commitment to fully implement the Uluru Statement during his victory speech in 2022.

Aboriginal and Torres Strait Islander tribes were the first sovereign Nations of the Australian continent. They possessed it under their laws and customs more than 65,000 years ago.

What is a Voice to Parliament?

The Voice would be a national group of about 20 Aboriginal members and Torres Strait Islander people. This body would be a balanced mix of genders and include a Youth and Disability Advisory Group. The Voice would advise Parliament on matters that are important to improve the lives of Indigenous Australians. This national group will remain, in place, even with government changes, as The Voice will be enshrined in the Constitution.

How would the Constitution change?

With three sentences to the Constitution. Here is the proposed draft wording (it's yet to be finalised because any constitutional change requires significant legal work).
1. There shall be a body called the Aboriginal and Torres Strait Islander Voice.
2. The Aboriginal and Torres Strait Islander Voice may make representations to Parliament and the executive government on matters relating to Aboriginal and Torres Strait Islander peoples.

3. The Parliament shall, subject to this Constitution, have the power to make laws concerning the composition, functions, powers and procedures of the Aboriginal and Torres Strait Islander Voice.

In 1967, First Nations people were counted. In 2023, Aboriginal and Torres Strait Islander people seek to be heard! Australia's First People invite you to walk with them in a movement of the Australian people for a better future for all!

The time is now to come together for our future generations to live in a Nation where everyone has the same opportunity to thrive. Empowering Aboriginal and Torres Strait Islander people to be self-determining, provide advice and offer input on the policies and legislation that affect them will support stronger outcomes for happier, healthier people and communities.

I will continue to share my stories through my artwork to help amplify the voices of our mob and to fight for a more fair and equitable place for our future generations! I have hope!

About the Author

Contemporary Australian Indigenous Artist with ancestral bloodlines to Ngarabal Nation and the Torres Strait Islands, Lauren is a self-taught artist who began painting at a very young age and has always loved creating! Art is an important platform for Lauren to share her Indigenous culture, and she hopes her art stirs your imagination and curiosity. Lauren hopes people connect with the stories behind her work to educate about First Nations' culture, history, stories, and language.

Lauren's artistic vision and inspiration come from the changing landscapes from her adventures around the Country. Lauren uses layers of fine dotting, line work, colour gradients, and Aboriginal symbolism/iconography and enjoys painting her works intuitively. Lauren loves to use bright colours that show extreme contrast and capture imagination. Lauren lives with her family in sunny Brisbane, Australia.

Website: www.laurenrogersarts.com
Email: laurenrogers@laurenrogersarts.com
Instagram: www.instagram.com/lauren_rogers_art_

Lauren Smith

Whoever has a heart full of love, always has something to give.

Jake and I were best friends who fell in love in our late teens. Our lives were typical of that age - we both worked full-time, I studied part-time and we loved to travel. Life was good. We got married young and had the world at our feet. We were so excited to carve out a life together. Life had other plans and four months into married bliss, Jake became severely unwell. There was a month of extreme agony and a whole host of symptoms before he was given a rare, aggressive lymphoma diagnosis. Not at all how we planned to start our lives together.

The following ten months were intense as Jake underwent ten rounds of various chemotherapy and seemed to experience the worst set of side effects after each one. I became his full-time carer and we juggled the balance of nurturing our relationship as husband and wife whilst also having to accept the patient/carer relationship that had been thrust upon us.

Jake's pain and suffering for 10 months was never my hope. Yet in that pain and suffering, I had the privilege to hold his hand and learn to be the best wife and carer I could be. We grew together in ways we never imagined. We got to spend every day together and face each challenge together. We got to cling to each other in the hardest days of our lives. That's a gift.

In January, hospitals were a foreign place to us and by October, we had lived in hospitals for more time than we had our home. I didn't ever dream of our home being a hospital room with constant interruptions.

The circumstances of 2019 were a huge set of things I never dreamed of or hoped for us. Yet, amongst all of the hard, we did have the opportunity to dream about one thing together - The dream for Heartfull.

As our life had been tipped upside down and stripped of anything normal, there was no doubt we needed a supportive community around us, however, despite there always being good intentions from our community, we did struggle with the complexities that our circumstances brought to our existing relationships.

We knew there was an abundance of people who would help us if we asked and had often said to us, "let us know if you need anything". The problem was that when I suddenly needed to ask for help, I wasn't sure who would be available or willing and I would end up being too afraid to ask.

I specifically remember one day as I was doing the washing (which is extra important when going through chemotherapy due to the cytotoxins), I realised we needed washing powder and I couldn't just pop out to get some as Jake couldn't be left alone with his specific care needs. I remember thinking that there were so many people who had offered help previously, but who would genuinely be free and willing to buy washing powder for me today and drive it out to me.

I thought to myself, wouldn't it be amazing if there was a tool that helped navigate these things, and the vision for Heartfull sparked. See, the love and willingness to help was there from friends and family, and the need was there, but there was a gap between the two. I shared my thoughts with Jake and together, we dreamed about how we would create Heartfull. A free app, that could be used when facing any of life's challenges, to bridge the gap between those willing to help and those who need it. It was nice to think that we could use the learnings and frustrations from our cancer experience to one day make other people's lives slightly easier.

I vividly remember that night, lying in bed with Jake until the early hours of the morning, chatting and dreaming about all the features we wanted to incorporate in Heartfull. It was not only an incredibly special thing to dream about the future with Jake whilst in the midst of an indefinite cancer journey, but it was also so lovely to share the same bed that night. It was a rare opportunity due to the cytotoxicity of chemo and the severe pain he suffered. I really treasure that memory.

As the months went on, I had a little notebook that was dedicated to notes about Heartfull. Every time we were off to the hospital for long days or stays, Jake would check that I had the notebook to continue working in it.

We endured 10 months of Jake fighting hard while I cared for him full-time, before he graduated to Heaven on 19 October 2019. He was 22. I became a widow at 21.

One of Jake's parting wishes to me was that I bring Heartfull to life. It was an honour to be able to carry that wish. Jake had the biggest heart for people. He had a gift for encouraging people so well, despite his own challenging circumstances.

Our dreaming meant that the mission for Heartfull was laid out for me, I just had to figure out how to bring it to life in Jake's honour.

Growing up, I always loved helping others – it made my heart happy. This was paired with my quiet, people pleaser personality which very much avoided any sort of spotlight attention. I was happy to go unnoticed, and that was still the case as an adult. However, the Heartfull mission was clear, and I needed to develop my character to equip me for the role.

My first hurdle was, I had no idea how to approach designing and building an app. In February 2020, I had my very first meeting about Heartfull. I was investigating what I needed to do from a trademark and intellectual property aspect. To most, that sounds like a basic meeting. To me, it felt like a scary job interview. My appointment wasn't until the afternoon and I spent all morning feeling sick, sitting with my nerves. It was the first time I was going to share our dream with someone and take steps to bring it to life. Thankfully, the meeting was great and so the journey began, to create Heartfull and to be a founder that could carry the dream to fruition.

The years since that first meeting in 2020 have been full of learning. There have been plenty of "one step forward, two steps back" moments as I fumbled my way through step by step and found the right people to support me along the way, and plenty of uncomfortable "spotlight" moments too. While public appearance is still not an easy thing for me, what is easy is knowing what I want for Heartfull. So, for the greater good of the dream, I have learned to embrace the uncomfortable moments and stretch myself. In fact, my word for the year in 2021 was "uncomfortable". It was a challenge and commitment to myself to make a conscious effort to say yes to the uncomfortable moments and opportunities. I squirmed at the thought of all the yeses I knew I would have to say as I chose the word, but I also knew that it was absolutely worth it in the pursuit of something that will alleviate some of the discomfort felt by others because of their circumstances. Jake didn't have a say in his severe discomfort for 10 months. So many others are also suffering discomfort. The least I could do was be uncomfortable more, for the benefit of Heartfull.

The peacekeeper in me has had to learn to navigate tough conversations to advocate for the core values of Heartfull, to campaign for a holistic user experience to be prioritised, and to identify when things are or are not serving the future of Heartfull well.

Funding has certainly been a significant challenge faced. Setting up a not-for-profit is no easy feat. In a commercial world, it is hard to establish something that primarily does good, for little return. I wanted to show that I backed myself completely, so for a long stretch of the journey I have completely funded this venture myself.

It was important to me that I put my money where my mouth was and invest in the future of Heartfull. I have now reached a point where it is time to seek funding opportunities to carry the app through the final development stage and launch. The scoping and design phases have been completed, and we are now ready to commence the development phase when funds allow.

Learning to hold all of this in tandem with the rolling waves of grief that wash over me has also been a journey. Having to choose time and time again to hold onto the hope of using our experiences for the benefit of others instead of allowing the grief to swallow me whole. Ultimately though, I refuse to let cancer ruin two lives. What pulls me out of those waves is my heart's desire to see Jake's legacy live on.

I am so grateful for all the people I have come into contact with on this journey and for the people who affirm my vision. *Sunrise* very kindly shared Heartfull's story in late 2021. The story had been on the local news the night before and I was very grateful for that, and I didn't actually know that it would also be picked up by *Sunrise*. Early in the morning, when the story reached the hearts of *Sunrise* viewers, my phone began to vibrate constantly. People were starting to follow Heartfull, they were signing up to stay in touch so that they'd be first to know when we launch, they were emailing me to share their life challenges and where they could see Heartfull would have helped in their world, and they were so kind in affirming the vision Jake and I had. It was very special to hear real people share the impact Heartfull would have.

Voices of Impact

A few of the many comments I received:

I completely agree that it is easier to ask a stranger for help than a family member and this is perfect. I can't wait for this app to take off and help those in need.

I am familiar with that moment when you just need washing powder. When you need to reach out for a helping hand without feeling needy or like you will owe someone. It's hard when you're alone. I have raised two small grandchildren, whilst looking after my physically disabled son, and having my own health challenges. I remember a time when they all got sick (vomiting) all at once. The washing was piled high. I ran out of washing powder, carpet cleaner and toilet paper. Far from ideal in the circumstances, but I couldn't leave the house. This app is such a great gift in being a practical helping hand for those with their own version of "spew mountain".

Thank you for this app that will help so many!!!

Bless you for this project. As recently diagnosed with a terminal illness I fully appreciate the great need for this type of thoughtful support.

My son is palliative. I don't know how to ask for help. I think this app is a beautiful notion.

As a mum in a FIFO family, I would love to rely on a support tool like Heartfull for those unexpected times.

My hubby died after a long 5 years of illness. I too remember the times I couldn't leave him alone and had no food here. Sometimes even just some milk for a coffee would have made my day. This is such an amazing idea. Now that I think about it, I can see the need for Heartfull in so many scenarios.

I have been in this position with my husband undergoing chemo and it is just a fabulous idea. I just wanted to wish you every success with its launch and look forward to seeing others supported by your app.

Lauren, as a single mum of three children with disabilities who can't be left alone, this idea is amazing. Thank you.

As we launch and grow, the hope and dream is to have a ripple effect. That the quiet dream of ours to make the weight of a cancer journey lighter for someone, will have spread around the nation and meet people in their times of need. That Heartfull will become a household name that can be relied upon when challenges arise.

To join us on our mission and be the first to know when launch time comes, please visit our website to sign up at www.heartfull.com.au.

You may not resonate with our story through a cancer journey. In fact, I hope you don't resonate with it. I wouldn't wish a cancer experience on anyone. However, I am sure you can resonate with other life challenges, and the times when someone has said to you, "let me know if you need anything", and accepting that help has been an uncomfortable thought.

Have you or someone you know struggled with post-natal depression? Heartfull could lighten the weight of the practical burden during that season.

Have you or someone you know experienced a tough pregnancy? Heartfull can rally your village during that season. Does your partner work away from home for periods at a time? Heartfull can be your safety net for those times when you inevitably need a helping hand with the kids.

Do you have an elderly parent who lives in a different city/state to you? Heartfull can coordinate support for them when you're unable to be around.

Have you or someone you know ever been in an accident that flips your world upside down and suddenly, a need for help through the rehabilitation season arises? Heartfull can ensure you are supported throughout that and can even assist in accelerated hospital discharge in some cases.

Do you or someone you know battle mental health challenges? Heartfull can provide a village of support for you when you need it, and more specifically, in the way you need it.

Have you ever lost someone close to you and had to ride the waves of grief? Heartfull allows your village to stand by you in those waves.

It's no secret that life is full of ups and downs. Everyone faces their own set of challenges and circumstances. Let's be a society that acknowledges this and advocates for leaning on the support of your community through those times. Surely, we would all benefit from extra kind-hearted moments weaved through the challenging seasons.

About the Author

Lauren Smith is the founder/director of Heartfull, a tool designed to bridge the gap between those happy to help and those who need it. Lauren has a wealth of personal experience in challenging life situations, in particular the cancer journey of her late husband. Heartfull was a project that they dreamed about while navigating this journey. The tool is completely versatile and can alleviate some of the burdens of whatever challenge life has thrown at you. After featuring on news platforms around the country, there has been an abundance of people sharing their stories and how Heartfull would change their world.

Some of Lauren's deepest values are people and making the most of life. She enjoys quality time with friends and family, striving for a meaningful work/life balance, and the place her soul feels most at home is by the ocean.

Email: hello@heartfull.com.au
Website: www.heartfull.com.au
Facebook: www.facebook.com/heartfullofficial

Melanie Wood

You Can't Delegate Communication

Would you like to become a fear–*less*, communicator in areas of your life?

It's time to stop being the best-kept secret and to Step Up, Step Out and Lead!

Lead yourself to lead others and create change in the world, to feel empowered to share your voice.

Whether it is to promote yourself in your business, in your organisation to help others, speak up at a meeting or speak up in your community. To have conversations with your loved ones and really communicate your needs, and to give permission for other women to do the same.

I'm here to guide you through my knowledge and experience of heart and mind coherence to help you use your voice and help you gain clarity and confidence to share more about who you are and what you do.

Beautiful lady, you can become the person in your vision that you have for yourself and your future!

I ask you to be open-minded and ready to take action in this chapter. As we begin, I want you to read through the steps and take a moment to start experiencing heart and mind coherence:

1. With your eyes open, begin to focus your attention on your heart
2. Breathing in slowly and deeply, focusing your attention on your heart and chest area, begin to feel love, care, compassion, and a sense of ease for yourself and continue to hold that feeling for 30 seconds
3. When you're ready to come back to the present moment. Remember that this simple 30-second technique can support you every time you want to reconnect with your heart!

How do you feel? Can you feel those feelings in your heart? I would like you to remember this tool throughout this chapter, and when in times that you feel fearful, anxious, or stressed – always come back to your heart and focus on that simple technique to re-centre yourself.

Opening my heart again after years of closing it down hasn't been an easy road and is still a work in progress today. I feel like if I fully surrender to my heart; I will lose control and be back in the situations I have worked so hard never to be in again. When I do connect to my heart it feels like home and I am me again. The HeartMath Institute and the people I have worked with have helped and supported me to continue to do the work every day and to surrender a little more each time.

Let's go back to before I was doing any of what I am currently doing today. I never set out to do any of the work that I currently do as a speaker, publisher, author and business owner. It sort of found me! Throughout my life, public speaking was never on my horizon. I would avoid it throughout school and my career for almost thirty years – and I did very well to avoid it at all costs! Maybe, you relate?

During my work career, going for interviews and having to do presentations, I would just feel so much stress, anxiety and fear leading up to it; during and after that, I would be too exhausted. The anxiety was all I could focus on in an interview or presentation or meeting – what was I going to do when it was my turn to speak up?

As it evolved, I became very good at procrastination. Placing my attention on it always made the fear worse. Feelings inside echoed constantly – my lack of self-worth, self-doubt, and feeling like I'm an imposter, would start to show in my external body. Sweaty palms and armpits would dictate what I could wear on those days as I needed to cover it up and hide, even though I lived in Scotland, where it was generally cold all the time.

My go-to way to hide the red blotchiness on my chest and neck was to pile on a lot of makeup and wear a turtleneck jumper (just as well I was living in cold Scotland at that time). How exhausting, right?

It didn't end there. I would have shaky hands, shaky legs, dry throat, and brain fog, and I wouldn't know what I was going to say next. I hated those situations, and even though I knew how to do the job, I found it difficult to get that across in a concise manner that actually makes sense. I received so many knockbacks from jobs because of this – which didn't help how I felt afterwards or encourage me to keep going. I felt like giving up. I didn't want to face those feelings of humiliation and embarrassment again. Nor rejection and failure. Have you ever felt like this in your life? Whether in a business organisation or communicating with people in groups?

During these times, I was also facing my biggest challenge of being in an abusive marriage. All in all, I lost my confidence, my voice, my certainty, my way in life and who I was as a woman… to the point I didn't want to be here.

One day, one person came along and gave me hope. She reached out to me and asked me if I was okay, and for once, I said, "No." She is the reason I'm here and why I do what I do every day.

She shared her own story with me and gave me hope and support for a year during which I left that marriage. After meeting her, I knew that I wanted to help other women overcome challenges and find their voice, confidence, and certainty around who they are, but I was still stuck.

I discovered that deep within that, I resented so much about my life that happened by following my heart and falling in love, getting married and throwing away a one-way ticket to America while it was my childhood dream to emigrate to another country. I threw so much away for love. I was so, so angry and frustrated at myself for that, and it continued for twelve years. Every day blurred into one, and the only thing that changed was that I put all my focus into my career to put a band-aid over what I had experienced and sweep it under the carpet.

For twelve years, I was frozen and had no idea of how to do what I wanted. But soon, everything changed with an opportunity to move to Australia.

One day, an opportunity to go to Australia for a year with my best friend knocked at my door. I really wanted to go; however, everything I had built in my life till then – home, car, secure job, pensions, savings – everything seemed against me!

Something within told me it was time for my adventure to begin, and this was what I had been waiting for. Prior to leaving, I was given the book "The Secret" by Rhonda Byrne.

Have you read that book before?

This was the first book I had read that wasn't Enid Blyton. I had never been exposed to ideas of self-development and spirituality before.

This book, The Secret, was telling me to take responsibility for my life. After the things that have happened to me in my life – I immediately rejected the idea. I remember thinking, "I didn't ask for all of those things to happen in my life. This is BS!".

I literally returned the book back to my friend, commenting about how I felt, and she told me to read it again, but with an open mind.

Well, I didn't want to be thought of as closed-minded, so I read it again and watched the documentary. Something inside me deeply shifted.

Arriving in Australia, I was ready! Ready to take action! Even though I was scared…so scared of being in a new country. Over the past almost 10 years in Australia, I have moved around a lot due to visas, love, debt and covid; it has been hard to feel settled;

renting for so long and packing and moving is tough on our mental wellness and physical wellness.

During this time, I decided to start a business, well I believe I was pushed into that direction after collapsing at work and ending up in the hospital for emergency surgery, yes it was the sledgehammer that brought me to my knees and I knew something had to change, I wasn't happy in the jobs I had been in. I knew the industry I was in needed to change, and every time I create change, I was brought down that change didn't need to happen and I was made out to be the troublemaker for stepping up and using my voice. I soon realised to make the difference I wanted to make, and this would need to be out of being in a job. Which at the time was a foreign concept, not growing up with business people or it was possible for someone like me, who dropped out of school at 15yrs and falling most of my exams and was told I would never amount to anything. This gave me the drive to prove them wrong.

Within a few months of leaving the hospital, I quit my job after an incident at work; with an even bigger push, I quit with no real plan, but with trust and slamming the door shut on any plan B, it was plan A. I started small, as a part-time business in Central Queensland, combining working in event management. My very first clients were speakers at these events, where I felt I could further develop speaking skills to be able to go on and make a greater difference in the lives of others.

And that's when *Speaking Styles,* my business, was born. The referrals started there, and after a year, I took the fledging business into a full-time flight! I took my past pain and turned it into my passion and purpose.

I wanted to help women like you (amazing lady reading this book!) have a voice, to have confidence, and clarity and be able to use your authenticity to create and build a skill set for you and your business and your life or represent your organisation through storytelling, public speaking and communication.

I worked with many coaches; I undertook many programmes around public speaking communication and mindset in order to be where I am today, helping women like you.

To help with speaking, mindset coaching would have to be a part of the process in a results-driven way, using tried and tested remedies, tools and techniques to overcome stress, anxiety, fear and uncertainty.

I was still looking to learn more – what does it take to be the most heartfelt communicator one can be? Learning about this to help women like you became my goal.

I dived into neuroscience; I took The Heart Math Certificate of "Clinical Certification for Stress, Anxiety and Emotional Regulation" to understand how to leverage the connection between the heart, body, and mind.

This helped me answer the key questions that better arm me to guide clients – what mental and emotional processes underlie this stress? How can we catch the onset of these feelings and patterns which support fear, stress and anxiety in us? And once we catch them, how can we successfully overcome them?

Today, the skills that I teach clients and women like you are Mindset, Authenticity, Storytelling, Communication/Speaking and becoming a best-selling author. Whether it is with your business or organisation to gain clarity, and confidence, overcome imposter syndrome and deal with overwhelm and or confusion around who you are.

How long have you known that you would like to be able to share more about yourself and what you do to help others? I want you to note that down right now. And then I want you to note down what is holding you back?

Is it fear of rejection? Failure? Humiliation? Fear of judgement? Or maybe even the fear of success?

My question for you is, how long have you been limiting yourself?

Jenny was an executive leader in a company with the CEO as her manager.

During her time in the company, she always felt in meetings that nobody was really listening to her, she didn't feel confident she felt really uncertain about really who she was and what she was there to do with communication with peers and team members. She would panic going into meetings, waffle while reporting and have multiple questions throughout as people didn't understand her.

Along the way, losing her confidence through the workplace and in past life events, how she communicated was a large part of her day and she reached out to me for help. Working together, her confidence increased. She was able to be clearer, she had more certainty going into her meetings, she had more clarity, and people were starting to respect her and listen to her. Actually, more work was getting done for herself and her team everybody was being more productive.

But here's the real special part of working together and helping her achieve this amazing turnaround in her life and her workplace. Jenny always felt she and the CEO didn't see eye to eye and that he didn't respect her the same as the other executives, constantly talking over her and crossing her boundaries. During our work together in the first couple of months, and how to structure having difficult conversations and apply them with the team. Jenny knew it was time to step up, step out and lead in this area. Jenny took the time to plan and prepare the meeting using the mindset tools and use the resources I had shared with her. She had a 40-minute meeting with her CEO and had all her notes in front of her; she even had "breathe" and "pause" in her notes, as well (another tool I teach with communication). She commanded respect; she set her boundaries. Detached from her emotions (anger, frustration, annoyance), and she was neutral in her approach to be able to get the outcome that she wanted. Jenny had no attachment to the outcome of whatever happened. She just knew that she had to do the meeting.

The CEO listened to her every word, she held her own throughout and her relationship with the CEO changed from that day forward. The CEO handed in his resignation to leave 2 days later (wow), and in the two weeks of his notice, they had the best working relationship; why? because she stood up for herself. She was on top of the world and said I have my confidence back; thank you for everything. When he left, they stayed in touch and he called her to be his advisor/consultant to help him in his next journey and venture that he was going embark on.

Jenny got the result we had been working on with confidence, clarity and communication.

It is so rewarding that clients that I have worked with have transformed their jobs into new ones and achieved personal and professional growth with return on investments emotionally and financially. Now, they are helping people in their fields do what they love to do. They are leading productive meetings with clarity, confidence, and compassion and giving permission for other people to do the same. They have a focus and vision about who they are, what they do, and where they're going from just a few short sessions with me.

I continue to work one on one with clients to gain clarity and confidence in their businesses and workplace. My passion is storytelling; from my own experience of how storytelling can save lives, heal ourselves and impact others, Voices of Impact Publishing was born in 2022 to help women feel empowered to share their stories and create change and give permission for other women to do the same. I have helped hundreds of women share their stories online, on stage, on podcasts and in their workplaces. To become Best-Authors giving them credibility, brand positioning and authority that can springboard their businesses and make an impact globally.

If you're here reading this – It's your time to shine just like the women here in this book.

Now, what's holding you back?

It is time for your adventure to begin. Become that fear–*less* speaker you have always visualised yourself to be using these programmes.

Stories are for sharing. For engaging and connecting with people. When we share stories, we save lives, just like how my friend did with me in Scotland. It can transform lives, and the effect is it ripples out into the world to help so many more people!

Getting up every single day and hearing the amazing results the women I work with are achieving keeps me going and, more importantly, makes me want to do more! To study more and grow personally and professionally. I love helping the many women that I have helped; the impact so far is greater than I could ever have imagined.

Imagine you are sharing your message and a story about the work you do. Close your eyes and imagine what does that feel like? What does it look like to you? Now write it down.

This is the beginning of your vision for you. My vision for you, for where I am going to go and take you, is to be able to help women to empower and inspire change in their life and in the lives of others.

By sharing your story, by communicating your message, by communicating your amazing work, experience, and expertise, no matter what field you are in.

My big vision is to be leading from the front as a speaker and publisher to be able to help more people around the world. For me, my dream and my vision are to impact globally, whether it's online or in-person, to really transform and help women feel empowered to share their stories. Having clarity and confidence and giving people permission to do the same.

Don't wait like I did to be ready, you're as ready as you can be now.

Time to stop being the best-kept secret! Remember that I believe in you and have your back. I would be very excited to go on this adventure with you, working together to help you become a fear—*less* speaker and storyteller. You are enough, just as you are.

Let's go and uncover the fear—*less* woman you are.

About the Author

Melanie is the owner of Speaking Styles Pty Ltd and Voices of Impact Publishing, specialising in Storytelling, Public Speaking and Mindset. Born in Scotland, now residing in Queensland, Australia. She is an International Speaker, Best Selling Author and Publisher. Melanie has empowered, inspired, and changed hundreds of female business owners, managers, and leaders to gain clarity and confidence to share their stories through writing and speaking.

Featuring on global platforms online and in person, Melanie's work and the story she shares, has been life-changing to the people she speaks to, meets and works with. She has also been featured in the World media including FOX, NBC, CBS, The Boston Herald, and NY Headline as the leading speaking coach Inspiring women to feel empowered to use their voice. Melanie loves to study mind-body connection in her spare time, as well as daily walks on the beach while living on the Gold Coast, Queensland.

Email: melanie@speakingstyles.com.au
Facebook/Instagram: @melaniewood
Website: www.speakingstyles.com.au

www.ingramcontent.com/pod-product-compliance
Lightning Source LLC
Chambersburg PA
CBHW050306010526
44107CB00055B/2118